THE GATHERING TABLE

By: Kathy Mitrano

RECIPES TO BRING FAMILY, FRIENDS AND MEMORIES TOGETHER

© 2018 by Kathy Mitrano All rights reserved.

Words Matter Publishing
P.O. Box 531
Salem, Il 62881
www.wordsmatterpublishing.com

No part of this publication may be reproduced, stored in a retrieval system, or transmitted in any way by any means—electronic, mechanical, photocopy, recording, or otherwise—without the prior permission of the copyright holder, except as provided by USA copyright law.

ISBN 13: 978-1-947072-46-6
ISBN 10: 1-947072-46-3

Library of Congress Catalog Card Number: 2018930168

DEDICATION

When I decided to compile a book of my favorite recipes, not only mine but favorite recipes from family and friends. I dug deep down into my heart and questioned even my intentions as to WHY was this important to me. The first person that came to my mind was my Mother. She rarely ever bought precooked meals, frozen dinners or fast food burgers!

My mom was graced with nine beautiful children ranging in ages from birth years from 1947 all the way to 1967! She always made sure there was a meal on the table a minimum of 3 times a day. She worked hard at home as well as outside the home. My father was a lifer in the United States Navy and how they managed to feed and clothe us for all these years still baffle me.

My dad passed from this earth in 1969 at the early age of 42 yrs. young. I was the second youngest of 9 siblings, and to this day, I still do not understand how we survived all that was handed to us on that platter. I do know, we rarely ever turned our nose up to whatever dinner was on the table. If we did, we would not eat (eventually, though, we came down off that high horse to fill our belly's!)

Our siblings all grew up and developed into young boys and girls, but not without those problems that any family with a 2-parent family. I guess our only difference was we didn't have that two-parent discipline from both parents.

I will admit, for the most part, sadly enough, there were times we took advantage of our disciplines!

And again, sadly, we saw how she struggled and at times seemed to lose parenting skills by us not obeying her. Many times, I wish I could turn that clock back and be the child that listened, and obeyed and helped much more than I did.

Mom was a great cook and always encouraged us not by doing for us, but by her guiding hand and her step by step lessons. She never criticized us for our mistakes, but made sure we learned from them! The days in the summer months, I cherish the times we went into farmer fields that you picked your own, and we would pick, the green beans, strawberries, rhubarb, corn, etc. I think all my five sisters can remember apple picking in the fall months and at least one occasion, we (her, myself and my young brother) missed the bus to take us back to the barn to weigh and pay. Now, now, my mom's sense of humor came out, and it was well worth being lost in the orchard! I will never forget, we were walking and she started singing "The Old Rugged Cross." That hymn and lyrics did get us to the next horse buggy, and we made it home safely.

So many other memories I could go on, but, this is a dedication to her and her efforts to make sure we had our food groups and healthy meals.

So, with just a few memories of the fall months and picking pumpkins and gourds, I

feel honored to be able to pass these on not only to my grandkids, my son and his wife. I think we, speaking for all my siblings, have been truly blessed by my mother! I will by no means stop at just her for this dedication as I much include my father for sadly passing at age 42 and left my mom with a shoulder of responsibility when it came to raising, then seven children still at home ranging in ages from 17 to age 2.

Mom passed over to be with my dad when she was 84 yrs. old. There is not a day that goes by that I find something in my daily living that carries me throughout my day.

In closing, I just want to say a HUGE Thank You to my Mom for allowing me to fail and through failure, I learned without becoming frustrated or stressed out to the point of giving up and calling it quits.

If there is one bit of advice I could give to each and everyone else out there, find those memories from those loved ones that have left this earth before you. If for nothing else, know they are guiding you and helping you through those small errors, whether it be cooking, sewing, raising children, etc. Follow their guidance. THANK YOU, MOM, FOR ALL YOU HAVE DONE AND FOR BELIEVING IN ME.

Sincerely,

Kathy Mitrano

Mom on her 84th birthday!

IN APPRECIATION

I have heard it said in the past, that behind every author, there is that one person who proves to be an inspiration from the beginning. I must give all that to my husband, Paul. He is my cheerleader, my critic, my driving force and last, but not least, I can honestly say Paul will keep the fires lit under me! I could not even attempt this book without him on my side and giving me the encouragement I so often need.

When we met, I knew that he was everything I had ever wanted in a husband. He has built me up when I feel the cards were against me. If I have an illness, he is my healing spirit! He can be my toughest critic, but at the same time, he will gently offer suggestions.

Without his enduring love and most of all, his patience, he can make me see that what I think is the impossible, and turn it into many possibilities! He is my sounding board, my hero and he knows how to turn my frowns into smiles and gives me all the confidence I need to get things done.

Most of all, my love for him is endless! He is very brave by being my taste tester (some things are fabulous, other dishes, he will gently tell me they are not keepers)! Above all I respect him, love him, and value all his opinions albeit, good, bad, terrible and downright throw it in the trash. He shows me complete honesty, and I love him for that. He is stuck with me whether he likes it or not! (smile!) I think we both knew from the first time we met, we had a pretty good feeling, that we would carry out the rest of our days on this earth together.

Paul is indeed my soulmate, and he stands the test of bravery by not being afraid to sample some of my stranger dishes. He knows he won't hurt my feelings by telling me his true thoughts and he also lends a hand to help me figure out what is missing or what needs to be taken out. He completes my life and is there to help me pick up the pieces when need be. And of course, I am there for him as well. I can't imagine my life without him. My appreciation to Paul, for the love, support, being my taste tester and many times my dishwasher. I Love You Paul to the ends of the Earth and then some!

Your Loving Wife

Kathy

There is always room for one more at our "Gathering Table."

Hello! This is the start of what I would like to be a cookbook. I made a commitment to begin this on December 27, 2016, but as you see, I am a little late in that commitment date. So here is a collection of my favorite recipes along with photos of food, family, and friends. In a way, I feel food brings fun, family, and friends together and that is how I have tried to arrange this book. In doing this, I had tears and smiles and laughs of past times and present as well.

I first need to give my utmost thanks to Chrissy Stock for believing in me that I could actually do this. I have tossed around the idea for years, but always realized I would never be Rachael (Love her to pieces!) Giada, another favorite, but feel incompetent. I am a normal 59-year-old mother and grandmother with a very supportive husband, Paul, who so totally believes in what I cook, so with that in mind, I do take recipes I find, then fine-tune them with a special touch! Some were complete flops, others are requested at every gathering!

I came from a family of which I was the 8th of 9 siblings. Father was military, and I remember many meals in one pot from my mom. Those are embedded in my memories. She was Polish and German. My father was Irish and German, so we had a mish-mash of meals, and many table manners that if not followed, well… we paid for that by my dad's humorous punishments.

The Gathering Table

With all this in mind, I am sure some of these recipes are like those you find in church cookbooks, PTA cookbooks, but some are also my own take on such recipes. Enjoy the recipes as well as short and mostly humorous stories that may go along with the recipes I remember…. My biggest problem will be proper measuring, but I will give it my best shot!

NOTE: All the photographs I have included are from my own personal collection.

All recipes are those that were given to me by friends and family, and I just want to share that with you.

Happy reading and good luck cooking!

Kathy Mitrano

Kathy Mitrano

LIST OF RECIPES

MAIN DISHES 1

    APPLE PORK CHOPS 2

    BAKED SAUSAGE, SQUASH, AND NOODLES 3

    BARB'S CHICKEN & DUMPLINGS 4

    BBQ SHRIMP 5

    BRUSCHETTA CHICKEN BAKE 6

    CHARLIE'S CHICKEN ATLANTA 8

    CHICKEN & SHRIMP COUBION 9

    CREAMY CHICKEN 10

    EGGS IN A NEST W/TOAST & JELLY 11

    FOR THE BIRTHDAY GIRL! 13

    EGGPLANT PARMESAN 14

    FETA POUCH 16

    GARLIC & BUTTER PORK LOINS SMOTHERED IN GRAVY 17

    GERMAN SAUERBRATEN 19

    HALUSHSKI (HA LOOSH SKI) 20

    KARTOFLANE KLUSKI (RAW POTATO DUMPLINGS) 21

    HAMBURGER DISH WITH LEEKS 22

    ITALIAN NOODLE DISH 24

    JIM BURKES AWESOME GUMBO! 25

    LENTIL STEW 27

    MEATLOAF WITH AU GRATIN POTATOES 28

    MUSCA CHOLI & MEATBALLS 30

    NANA'S CHICKEN CACCIATORE 31

    REUBEN CASSEROLE 32

SALMON SPAGHETTI WITH CREAM SAUCE ... 33
SICILIAN MEAT ROLL (MEATLOAF) ... 34
SHRIMP ETOUFFEE ... 35
TACO'S ... 36
TAMALE PIE ... 37
TORTELLINI SOUP WITH SAUSAGE AND SPINACH ... 38

VEGETABLES AND SIDE DISHES ... **41**
BUTTERNUT SQUASH CASSEROLE ... 42
BUTTERNUT SQUASH MAC & CHEESE ... 43
CAULIFLOWER IN CHEESE SAUCE ... 45
CREOLE FRIED RICE ... 46
FRIED CORN ... 47
LAYERED SPAGHETTI SQUASH ... 48
ONION SHORTCAKE ... 49
SMOTHERED GREENS ... 50
SPECIAL BEANS ... 51
SPINACH AND RICE SIDE DISH ... 52
TWICE BAKED POTATOES ... 53
ZESTY CARROT BAKE ... 54
ZUCCHINI-POTATO CASSEROLE ... 55

SALADS ... **57**
BAKED SHRIMP & CRAB SALAD ... 58
BROCCOLI AND BACON SALAD ... 59
CREAMY FRUIT SALAD ... 60
DEE'S CABBAGE SLAW ... 61
FRESH BROCCOLI SALAD ... 62
ITALIAN RESTAURANT SALAD ... 63
MACARONI SALAD ... 64

    MATT'S YEARLY BIRTHDAY DINNER! 65

    STRAWBERRY ARUGULA SPRING SALAD 66

    PAM'S PASTA SALAD 68

    RICE ARTICHOKE SALAD 69

    SPINACH SALAD 70

DESSERT **71**

    ANGEL LUSH TRIFLE CAKE 73

    APPLE BETTY 74

    APPLE CRISP 75

    BAKED APPLES 76

    BANANA SPLIT DESSERT 77

    BETTER THAN ANYTHING CARAMEL CAKE 78

    BETTER THAN SEX CAKE 80

    CHOCOLATE OVERLOAD PEANUT BUTTER CAKE 81

    CHOCOLATE CAVITY MAKER CAKE 83

    CHOCOLATE COVERED CHERRY COOKIES 85

    COCONUT CREAM PIE 86

    CRACK CRACKERS 87

    CRANBERRY APPLE CRISP (LOW CAL.) 88

    CREAM CHEESE FROSTING 90

    HUMMINGBIRD CAKE 91

    MAPLE NUT BLONDIE WITH CREAM SAUCE 92

    MAPLE CREAM SAUCE 92

    OATMEAL RAISIN COOKIES 93

    ONE BOWL APPLE CAKE 94

    OREO TRUFFLES 95

    PAMELIA'S BACARDI RUM CAKE 96

    PECAN PIE CAKE 97

PEPPERMINT BARK RITZ BITES ... 98

RUM GLAZED ROASTED PECANS ... 99

SPRITZ COOKIES ... 100

WHITE CHOCOLATE CHIP AND DRIED CRANBERRY COOKIES ... 101

MISCELLANEOUS **103**

CEASER DRESSING ... 104

CHEESE DIP ... 105

CREAMY HORSERADISH DIP ... 106

DEVILED EGGS ... 107

GARLIC HERBED CHEESE BOMBS ... 108

HOME CANNED PINT SALSA RECIPE TO FOLLOW: ... 109

KALE SOUP ... 110

MARYLAND CRAB CAKES ... 111

MOM'S THUNDER AND LIGHTENING SALSA ... 113

RED PEPPER RELISH ... 115

SALSA ... 116

SPICY CORN DIP ... 117

SPINACH AND ARTICHOKE DIP ... 119

THICK & CREAMY NEW ENGLAND CLAM CHOWDER ... 120

WARM REUBEN DIP ... 121

SPICE REPLACEMENTS ... 122

MEASURING GUIDE ... 123

HOLIDAY HAPPINESS ... 124

WHITE CHRISTMAS ... 127

ABOUT THE AUTHOR ... 129

Growing up, my father was a lifer in the Navy… so when he said JUMP…. We said "Yes sir… how high?" Well, in reality, it wasn't that bad. We all remember our parents going to the base commissary for the monthly grocery run and we would see that station wagon driving up the lane and one by one we carried in the grocery bags. It seemed looking back now, it could have fed 5 families! But you had 8 children all under the age of 12. We have to laugh in conversations with my mom in later years that all those groceries totaled approximately $65.00! To feed 14 people for a month! Nothing and I mean NOTHING went to waste! Many one-pot meals and unlike this day and age a one-pot meal…was exactly that a ONE POT MEAL….. NO LEFTOVERS! A quick note here. Table manners were extremely enforced! No elbows on the table, no using fingers to scoop food on the spoons or forks, no chewing with the mouth open (Navy man at his best)! Now, for those infractions. Scooping food… we had to put our plate on the floor and eat as a dog would eat! Elbows on the table, we sat on the hand not being used! And opened mouth chewing…well, I can't quite remember the remedy for that!

The Gathering Table

I know I learned dearly the rules at the dinner table! I now have a son, 33 years old, and those manners are still passed on to my grandkids. (I must secretly smile, knowing I did do something right!) If there were vegetables, we absolutely despised… we were required to eat at least 2 (peas, corn, etc.). Although we had good table manners, we still found humor in them.

Enough reminiscing for now! Let's get to a few recipes that I can remember as a child (many years, so bear with me!)

APPLE PORK CHOPS

- 1 tablespoon butter or margarine
- 4 (4 oz.) bone-in pork loin chops
- Mrs. Dash seasoning
- 1 med. onion
- 1 cup apple juice
- 2 Granny Smith apples, peeled, cored and sliced

Melt butter or margarine in non-stick skillet. Add chops and brown lightly, about 2 minutes on each side. Sprinkle Mrs. Dash on chops and arrange onion slices on top. Pour apple juice into skillet. Bring to a simmer, cover and cook 25 minutes. Uncover and add apple slices to pan and cook 5 minutes. Serve chops with apple slices and pan juices. Serves 4.

BAKED SAUSAGE, SQUASH, AND NOODLES

- ✓ 2 tablespoons+1 teaspoon butter
- ✓ 2 tablespoons all-purpose flour
- ✓ 2 cups milk, warmed
- ✓ ½ teaspoon salt
- ✓ ½ teaspoon pepper
- ✓ 6 oz. goat cheese
- ✓ 2 tablespoons fresh sage, chopped
- ✓ ¼ lb. butternut squash, cubed
- ✓ 1 bag wide egg noodles
- ✓ 2 tablespoons Italian breadcrumbs
- ✓ 12 oz. turkey sausage (can also use chicken or even pork)

Heat oven to 350. Coat a 9x12 pan with cooking spray. Bring a large pot of lightly salted water to a boil. In a medium saucepan melt 2 tablespoons butter over medium heat whisk in flour and cook for a minute. Whisk in milk salt and pepper. Bring to a simmer for 2 minutes, whisking constantly. Remove from heat, add cheese and sage and set aside. To the boiling water add squash and cook for 4-5 minutes, stir in egg noodles and return to boil and cook 5 min. more. Drain. Meanwhile, melt the 1 teaspoon butter in a non-stick skillet over med. high heat. Add breadcrumbs and brown 30 seconds. Transfer to a bowl. Crumble sausage into the same skillet and cook for about 4 minutes breaking apart with a wooden spoon.

Transfer drained noodles and squash to a large bowl. Stir in cooked sausage and cheese sauce. Fold all together until well mixed. Pour into prepared baking dish evenly. Top with toasted crumbs. Bake at 350 for 20 to 25 minutes.

BARB'S CHICKEN & DUMPLINGS

This is one of my favorite dishes that Barb makes. I have tried to replicate it, and each time I try, I get a little better at it. My biggest problem was trying to get the dumplings the right consistency. Each time I visit, we will make it together, and I think I have come a long way since the first time! Enjoy, and unlike me, don't be intimidated! Ha ha!

- ✓ 1 whole chicken (enough water to cover) ** (I remove much of the skin to avoid a fatty broth)
- ✓ 1 large onion, cut into chunks
- ✓ 2-3 garlic cloves, coarsely chopped
- ✓ 2 stalks celery, sliced
- ✓ Salt and pepper to taste
- ✓ Parsley, fresh is best

Boil the chicken, onion, and garlic until the chicken is done. Remove chicken from pot, let cool and debone and cut into bite-size pieces. Be sure to taste your broth and if need be season accordingly. You may add chicken bouillon if you need more of a chicken flavor, just bc careful of the sodium content. Add celery and bring broth to a boil and prepare the dumplings as follows:

- ✓ 5 eggs, beaten
- ✓ 1 teaspoon baking powder
- ✓ Flour
- ✓ Splash of milk (if needed)

After eggs are beaten, add the baking powder and flour to make a smooth consistency of dough, but not runny. If it seems a little too dry add a splash of milk just to moisten. Once broth is boiling add teaspoonfuls of dough and boil unit floating. Add back in your cooked chicken, and Serve!

**If you have a preference for white or dark meat you can buy just those pieces and use chicken broth for more flavor while cooking. This is a translated recipe from Germany, and she had no real measurements, but I am the first to admit, it's an awesome pot of chicken and dumplings!

Kathy Mitrano

BBQ SHRIMP

- 3 slices of bacon chopped
- ½ teaspoon oregano
- ½ lb. butter or oleo
- 2 cloves garlic, crushed
- 2 tablespoons Dijon mustard
- 2 tablespoons crab boil
- 1 ½ teaspoons chili powder
- ½ teaspoon Tabasco
- 1/4 teaspoon basil
- ¼ teaspoon thyme
- 1 teaspoon black pepper
- 1 ½ lb. large shrimp**

Heat oven to 375 degrees. Fry bacon until crisp. Drain. Add butter and all other ingredients except Shrimp. Simmer 5 minutes. Place shrimp in a baking dish and pour sauce over the top. Stir to coat all the shrimp. Cook in the oven for approx. 20 minutes. **Remove tails before baking or keep them on and remove before eating. ENJOY!

Another small note on Dee. Of course, she is married to Paul's brother Don. She is a very talented person. She did dog training and has a love for ALL animals… (except frogs!). Even the squirrels will come down and take the peanuts from her hand. She is a modern-day version of Dr. Doolittle! She paints many things and is a true artist. She tried to show me… but to no avail. (I blame it on being left-handed!) She also does beading, jewelry and such. Her love is white tigers and is currently working on a tapestry of beading a white lion. It's done with very small beads and time-consuming. It so far is beautiful. She calms me when I am stressed, she is happy when I am happy, and my love for her and Donnie is unending. We have the pleasure when we visit to also see her sister Sandy and husband Al. I hate leaving once we get there! It is definitely a home away from home.

BRUSCHETTA CHICKEN BAKE

- 1 can (14.5 oz.) diced tomatoes, undrained***
- 1 pkg. Stove Top Stuffing Mix for chicken
- ½ cup water
- 2 cloves garlic, chopped
- 1 ½ lb. chicken meat, cut into bite-size pieces
- 1 teaspoon dried basil leaves
- 1 cup shredded mozzarella cheese

Heat oven to 400 degrees. Mix tomatoes, water, and garlic just until stuffing mix is moistened. ***I normally will use a can and a half of the tomatoes and normally I will buy the basil, garlic & oregano flavored diced tomatoes. Layer chicken and basil in the bottom of a 3 qt. casserole or 9x13 baking dish. Top chicken with the stuffing mixture and the mozzarella cheese evenly and I sprinkle a little more basil on top. Bake 30-40 minutes or until chicken is done.

I am not even sure where I got this recipe, and have not made it. As you know in the workplace, recipes get passed back and forth, and I am sure that is where it came from.

CHARLIE'S CHICKEN ATLANTA

Ingredients:

- ✓ 4 boneless, skinless chicken breasts (salt & peppered)
- ✓ 4 tablespoons honey mustard
- ✓ 2-3 chopped green onions
- ✓ 3-4 slices bacon, chopped, fried and drained well
- **fresh sliced mushrooms are a good option if you like them
- ✓ Shredded mozzarella cheese

Preheat oven to 350 degrees. Spray baking sheet to prevent chicken from sticking. Place chicken breast on a baking sheet and bake until chicken is no longer pink inside and internal temperature is 180 degrees. Remove from oven. Keep the chicken on the baking sheet, as it will have to go back in the oven after toppings are applied. Over each chicken breast, spread up to a tablespoon over each breast. On top of the honey mustard, sprinkled the crumbled bacon, green onion slices, and sliced mushrooms if added. Sprinkle each breast with the mozzarella cheese. Place baking sheet with topped chicken back to oven just long enough to get the cheese melted. Remove from oven and serve with your favorite vegetables and a rice side or potato. Enjoy the blend of flavors on the chicken!

This picture is myself and 4 of my sisters at a nephew's wedding. From the left: Me, Pam (the oldest sister), Janet, Cindy and Judy. (Judy and Janet are twins)

My friend Mary had the same love of cooking and collecting recipes that I have, and she has shared some of those with me through the years that we were neighbors.

CHICKEN & SHRIMP COUBION

- Approx. 2 lbs of boneless/skinless chicken filets

  (you may also cut the chicken into bite-size pieces for quicker cooking)
- 1 lb. bag of large shrimp, shelled and deveined
- 2 cups chopped onion
- 1 cup chopped green onion
- ½ cup chopped green pepper
- ½ cup chopped red pepper
- 3 cloves chopped garlic
- 2 cans tomato sauce
- 1 or 2 cans diced tomatos (I use my home canned quarts!)
- 1 small can tomato paste.
- Salt, pepper, hot sauce, Old Bay or Cajun seasoning.

Pour a small amount of oil just to barely cover the bottom of the pot and once heated, saute the onions, peppers, ½ of the green onions,

Add chopped garlic until onions are translucent. Add tomato sauce, canned tomatoes, and your tomato paste. Add about a half can of water from each tomato sauce can as well. Add your salt, pepper, hot sauce (or cayenne pepper) to your taste and some of the Old Bay. Simmer on low for 1-2 hours. You may want to add just a tad of sugar if the tomatoes have a tang to them. Stir as needed so as nothing is sticking to the bottom. After 2 hours add your chicken filets and shrimp. It's important NOT TO STIR! You can use pot holders and gently shake the pot if you stir, then the chicken will end up shredded! Cook for another 30-40 minutes or until chicken is done. Serve this up with some good sticky rice and its one tasty Cajun dish!)

Now all my recipes from my Louisiana friends seem like stews, soup and such. I did come up with a salad to go along with whatever we were eating. Not sure I would consider it "Cajun" but, it is an excellent addition to ANY meal. It's easy and made the day before and refrigerated overnight. DEFINITELY worth trying!

CREAMY CHICKEN

- ✓ 4 leg quarters
- ✓ 4 strips of bacon
- ✓ Dijon mustard
- ✓ 2 onions, sliced in rings
- ✓ 1 qt. heavy whipping cream
- ✓ Salt and pepper to taste
- ✓ Minced garlic (optional)

Salt and pepper your leg quarters. Coat with mustard, then wrap each one in a slab of bacon. Set chicken in a casserole dish. Spread your onion rings over the chicken. Pour the heavy cream over the chicken pieces and onion rings. Add minced garlic to taste. Bake in a 350 degrees oven for about 1 to 1½ hour, or until your chicken is done. This serves well over pasta such as linguini. (Makes 2-4 servings).

Another great Recipe from Barb. I truly appreciate her efforts trying to get all this translated from German to English!

Kathy Mitrano

EGGS IN A NEST W/TOAST & JELLY

- ✓ Raw Potatoes, peeled rinsed and shredded
- ✓ (1 per person or 2 if large potato)
- ✓ 1 egg per person per serving.

Shape the shredded potatoes into nice patties and lay gently in hot oil in cast iron or non-stick pan. Fry on medium heat and keep an eye on the bottoms and when lightly crisp or brown, gently flip and do the same to the other side. Remove from pan and removed centers of hash browns. For the eggs, crack them gently as to not break the yolk (I still am trying to master that part). When the egg is cooked, it will go in the center of the hash browns. Hot toast with jelly and a great Navy man's breakfast!

As time went on, he found one of us girls that could make him an awesome breakfast! That was her job on the weekends. Today she is 62 and still makes an awesome breakfast just as she did in her early teens!

This is an OLD picture of myself and my siblings taken at Christmas.

This was probably one of the last photos taken of Mom with all 9 kids in 2003.

As my sisters and I all became adults, we discovered that all have had the "Mom's cooking gene" within us. Six girls and three boys, and we all cook and are not afraid to try new things, and if it fails, we find out why and keep trying until we get it right. Now, I have three brothers, and there is one that OWNS his kitchen. When we go to visit, and he will tell me to cook something that he has perfected, I become frantically nervous! He is good about it though, as he will patiently guide me if I need guidance. However, he has a sense of humor about him that at times I have to guess if he is serious or not. He and his wife live in Anacoco, Louisiana, so he is teaching me some Cajun-style cooking. It's a little difficult sometimes due to the fact that my husband is from Massachusetts (a different country, according to my brother)! He is learning to like those dishes from my brother (especially when we are visiting with him, once we are back in IL, well… he tolerates it!)

FOR THE BIRTHDAY GIRL!

My Granddaughter, Kylie and I made this apron for "Mommy Nonna (Madonna)" as a birthday present. Kylie picked out the fabric, and I guided her on the sewing machine!

The twins, Collin and Ethan decided to make her cupcakes! They did all but put them in the oven. These were the large muffin cups we baked in!

Every year for my daughter-in-law, Madonna, I make her a special birthday dinner. It is now a tradition. She chooses what she would like from the apps to dessert! The Crab cake recipe was one of her favorites, and the following turned out to be a success. She decided she wanted eggplant parmesan. Okay! I searched and read about eggplant, what to look for, ripeness, etc. I am not even sure where I found the recipe, but I gambled a lot and tweaked it. I did a great job if I must say so myself!

EGGPLANT PARMESAN

- 2 lbs. eggplant (2 large)
    *Choose nice firm, if they are soft they may be somewhat overripe
- Salt
- 1 28 oz. can whole tomatoes
- 1-2 cloves garlic, minced
- olive oil
- ground pepper
- ½ cup flour
- ½ cup seasoned breadcrumbs
- 4 large eggs, beaten
- 4 cups shredded mozzarella cheese
- 1 cup grated fresh Parmesan
- 1 cup packed fresh basil leaves
    1 lb. ground Italian sausage, browned

Cut eggplant lengthwise into ¼ to ½ inch slices. Arrange one layer in the bottom of large colander and sprinkle evenly with salt. Repeat with all the eggplant. Cover with a paper towel and place a couple of plates on top (the weight of the plates will help the moisture be removed.) Let sit for approx. 2 hours. If you choose to use sausage in your sauce, now would be the time to brown the meat and drain all fat. Add tomatoes, minced garlic, salt, pepper and a drizzle of olive oil. Italian seasoning can be added as well for a more robust flavor. Let sauce simmer.

In a wide shallow dish combine flour and breadcrumbs and mix well. In another wide shallow dish add 4 beaten eggs.

In a deep skillet, pour enough olive oil in to cover bottom (about ½ inch or so). When the oil is shimmering, take your eggplant slices and dredge first in the dry mixture, then in the beaten eggs (this helps your breading stay on). Work in batches. Brown on both sides, being careful not to over fry or burn.

Preheat oven to 350 degrees. In the bottom of a glass baking dish (9x11) spread about a cup of sauce. Layer with eggplant slices. Top the eggplant with shredded mozzarella cheese, grated Parm cheese, and basil leaves. Keep layering as such. You should have 3 layers. The top layer of eggplant covered in mozzarella, grated Parm, and remaining basil leaves. Bake until cheese has melted, and the top is slightly browned (about 30 minutes). Allow to rest for 10 minutes before serving. Save some grated fresh Parm. for topping.

This was only my second attempt at making any type of eggplant, and it came out fantastic! I served this with a light Italian salad and yeast rolls. I found a recipe for these that made this a true birthday dinner!

FETA POUCH

- 8 oz. feta cheese (or goat cheese)
- 1 large or 2 Roma tomatoes
- ½ red onion
- 1 green pepper*
- 1 red bell pepper*
- 1 yellow pepper*
- Fresh mushrooms, sliced*
- 4 garlic cloves
- Jalapeno peppers (optional)
- Salt, pepper, Italian seasoning, parsley (fresh herbs are fantastic!)
- Extra virgin olive oil

*All peppers and mushrooms are optional and adjust to your own taste.

Heat oven to 400 degrees. Slice all the vegetables that you will be using. Line a sheet pan with foil and coat with olive oil. Lay out the cheese in the middle of the pan in a round shape. Layer the sliced vegetables over the top of the cheese. Season. Drizzle a little more olive oil, and you may need another piece of foil raise the edges and cover the cheese mix. Bake in the oven for 30 to 40 minutes or until vegetables are done (time will depend on how many vegetables you put on.) It can also be done for several individual servings as well. Remove from oven and carefully un-foil, so as not to get a steam burn. Enjoy. Goes well with garlic bread!

GARLIC & BUTTER PORK LOINS SMOTHERED IN GRAVY

- 2-4 thick-cut pork loin chops
- ½ stick butter
- 2 garlic cloves, minced
- ¼ cup flour
- ¼ cup milk
- 1 tablespoon oregano
- 1 tablespoon thyme salt & pepper to taste
- 1 cup fresh mushrooms, cleaned and sliced (I sometimes use more!)

Preheat your oven to 350 degrees. In a large skillet over medium-high heat, combine butter, garlic, mushrooms, and spices. Once the butter has melted, add your chops and sear on each side for about 1-2 minutes or until golden brown.

(They will finish cooking in the oven). If your skillet is oven-proof, place skillet in oven and bake for approx. 35 minutes or until centers are no longer pink. (If it is not ovenproof, I move them to a small baking dish for the oven). Remove skillet from oven and set chops aside to rest. Whisk flour and milk into the pan with the other ingredients until all lumps are removed. Simmer for about 3 to 5 minutes. Serve the gravy over the chops. ** I will sometimes up the amount of flour and milk to make a little more gravy, keeping the ratio correct. ** This serves very well with rice or mashed potatoes.

GERMAN SAUERBRATEN

- 1-2 lb. beef roast
- 2 cups beef broth
- 1 medium onion
- 1 rib celery
- 1 carrot
- 2 cloves garlic
- 2 prunes or raisins (optional)
- 1 teaspoon sour cream
- Salt & Pepper
- Paprika
- 1 tablespoon oil
- 1 tablespoon butter
- 1 tablespoon sugar

MARINADE

- 1qt. buttermilk
- 1/3 cup vinegar
- Several peppercorns
- 2 cloves garlic
- 1 bay leaf
- Pinch of sugar
- 1 large onion

For Marinade, mix buttermilk, vinegar, peppercorns, bay leaf, sugar, garlic (smash whole cloves with a knife) and onion (cut in wedges in a big pot. Bring to a boil. Turn off heat and let it cool. Add meat. If the meat is not completely covered with liquid, add water or vinegar. Refrigerate for 2 days.

Heat oven to 350 degrees. Take meat out of the marinade and dab dry with paper towel.

Season with salt, pepper and paprika. Heat oil and butter in Dutch oven. Add sugar on the edge and let it caramelize while browning meat on all sides. When meat is brown pour in broth. Put celery, carrots, med. onion (cut into wedges), garlic, and prunes or raisins (optional) around the meat. Cover and cook in the oven for 1 1/2 hours. Check and turn meat every half hour to keep it moist all over, add water if needed.

When done take meat out of the pan and let it rest. (I usually use the lid of the Dutch oven.) Put the gravy back on the stove, bring to a boil and thicken with flour. Let it cool until it is still hot, but not boiling and add sour cream. Season to taste with salt and pepper if needed. Slice meat and add back to gravy or serve separately. The veggies can be taken out of gravy, or left in, and served with the meal. Serve with German potato dumplings, Spätzle, noodles or potatoes, and red cabbage.

HALUSHSKI (HA LOOSH SKI)

A pound of pork Sausage links. Fried and sliced into bite-sized pieces

Save drippings and add a stick of butter and shred one head of cabbage. Fry in the butter and drippings. When cooked through, mix the sausage back in, you may want to use a larger pan in order to get it all thoroughly mixed.

Next step is making potato dumplings.

Another name for these is:

KARTOFLANE KLUSKI (RAW POTATO DUMPLINGS)

- ✓ 2 cups of raw potatoes
- ✓ 1 egg
- ✓ 1 teaspoon salt
- ✓ 1 1/2 cups flour

Grate potatoes fine; drain off brown liquid. Add the beaten egg, salt and flour to make stiff dough. Drop into boiling salted water from a wet spoon. Dumplings will float when finished and of course, remove. Use an extra-large dish and mix the sausage, fried cabbage and dumplings together and it is one dish that even as young children, we LOVED. Once I make it and mix it, I will usually put it in the crockpot on warm, just to let the flavors blend.

As I said, my father was a lifer in the U.S. Navy, and when he finally retired, we became his young sailors! We listened, followed orders and of course, all in the name of fun. He gave us our chores written on a board, and we would get a small allowance twice a week IF we did our chores as listed. Dad was most times the breakfast captain in the kitchen on the weekends mostly. For a large family, we had biscuits and gravy often, as well as Eggs in a Nest.

HAMBURGER DISH WITH LEEKS

- 2 large onions, chopped
- 1-2 cloves chopped garlic*
- 1 tablespoon butter or oil
- 1 lb. ground beef
- 3 oz. tomato paste
- 2 stalks of leek
- ½ cup beef broth
- 1 tablespoon mustard
- 1 teaspoon paprika
- 1 teaspoon salt
- 2 tablespoons sour cream

*Garlic is optional

Saute chopped onion and garlic in oil and butter. Add ground beef and brown. Drain any excess fat. Lower heat and add in sliced leeks, tomato paste, mustard, and seasonings. Simmer on low for about 15 minutes, stirring frequently. Add sour cream and serve. Pairs well with rice or egg noodles. (If you like more of a gravy, you can add more broth if needed).

Kathy Mitrano

Just a note: First time my husband (Paul) had this, and he liked it. I made it according to the recipe, but it has room to add ingredients. I would like to try mushrooms and peppers in it as well. Also, I think substituting the beef for pork sausage would taste just as great!

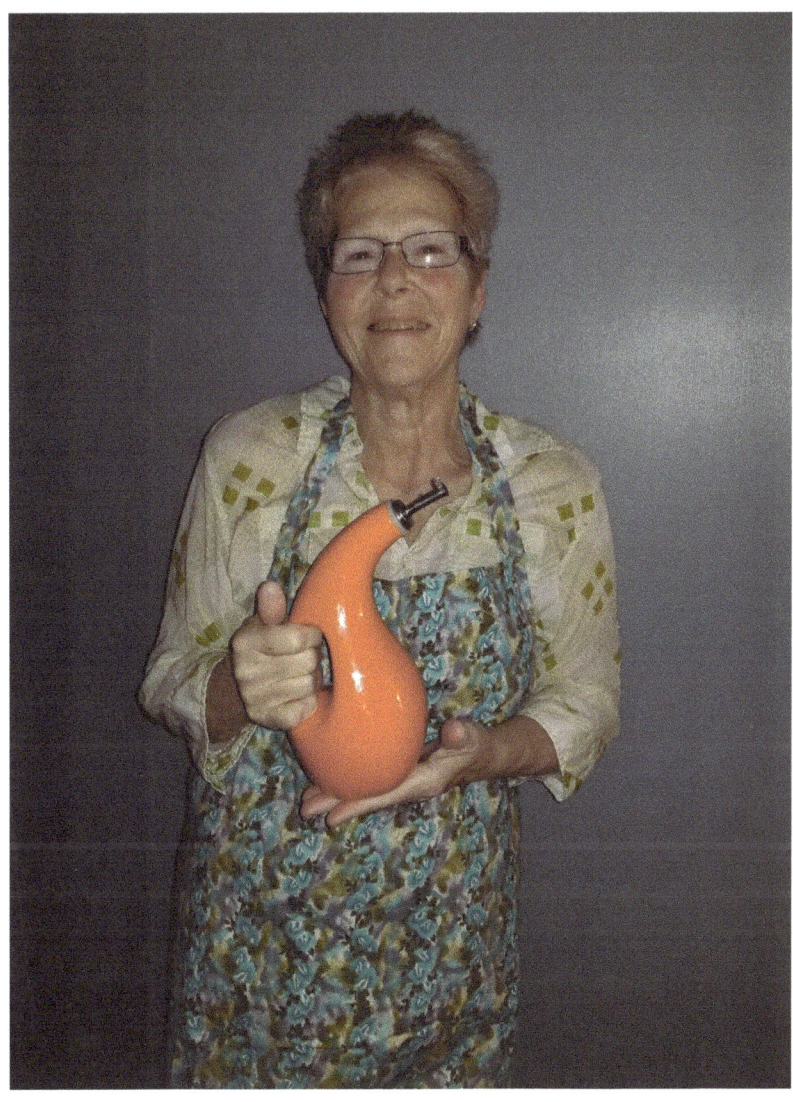

The Gathering Table

ITALIAN NOODLE DISH

This is another translated dish from Barb, and she has done her best in the translation!

- ✓ 1-12 oz bag flat noodles
- ✓ 1½ lb. ground beef
- ✓ 3 small cans tomato paste
- ✓ ¾ cup dry red wine
- ✓ 4-5 cloves garlic, minced
- ✓ ¾ pint heavy whipping cream
- ✓ 2 onions thinly sliced
- ✓ Pam or butter spray
- ✓ Cayenne pepper, salt, thyme, rosemary, oregano & parsley to taste.

Boil noodles. Set aside. Season ground beef with the cayenne pepper and salt. Add onions. Continue cooking until they are translucent. Remove from heat and add dry wine. Add tomato paste and season with thyme, rosemary, oregano, parsley, and garlic. Spray a baking dish, Layer noodles, ground beef mixture and top with another layer of noodles. Sprinkle with Parmesan cheese and the heavy cream. Broil until golden brown on top. This serves well with a nice green vegetable of your choosing.

Kathy Mitrano

JIM BURKES AWESOME GUMBO!

Cajuns "guarantee" a tasty experience

Ingredients:

- ¼ cup flour
- 1 teaspoon salt
- 2-3 chicken cut in 8 pieces**
  - ***I also add kielbasa sliced in 1 to 1 ½ slices as well*
- ¼ cup vegetable oil
- 1 ½ cups chopped onion
- 1 cup chopped celery
- 1 cup chopped green onion
- 3-5 cloves garlic, chopped
- 1 qt. broth
- 1 – 16 oz. can tomato, juice and crushed
- 1 bay leaf
- 1 teaspoon Tabasco sauce
- 1 10 oz whole okra, fresh or frozen, sliced
- 3 cups cooked rice, divided

Combine flour, salt in bag, dredge chicken in flour mix. In large Dutch oven, heat oil, brown chicken on all sides, remove and reserve, add onion, celery green onion and garlic to saucepot and saute five minutes, stirring often. Return chicken to pot, stir in chicken broth, tomatoes, bay leaf and Tabasco. Bring to a boil, reduce heat, simmer 45 minutes uncovered. Add okra and cook ten minutes longer. Serve each with rice and makes 6-10 servings. ** I will use the boneless thighs and breasts for my chicken, cut into pieces just to eliminate having to worry about the bones!

This is my first pot of gumbo I made on my own. I had to send a picture to my brother to let him see!

This is the best gumbo I have ever tasted, and My brother Jim gave me his stamp of approval once I made it. (Of course he was close by to guide me!)

I have been blessed to try a few other "Cajun" dishes which I will share with you as well.

LENTIL STEW

- 1 cup dry lentils
- 5 cups water
- 1 tablespoon butter
- 2 onions, diced
- 2 carrots, sliced
- 2 stalks celery, sliced
- 1 bay leaf
- 2 whole cloves
- ¼ teaspoon thyme (to taste)
- 1 lb. potatoes, diced
- ¼ lb. ham and bratwurst, kielbasa1 pkg. brown gravy mix (or any sausage to your liking) Even short ribs are good!
- 1 tablespoon tomato paste
- Splash of vinegar
- 1 teaspoon sugar

Saute onions until translucent or light brown. Add diced carrots, celery. Saute lightly. Add water, lentils, bay leaf, cloves, thyme and salt and pepper to taste. Cover and cook approx. 30 minutes or until Lentils are soft. Add potatoes and cook an additional 15 minutes, or until cooked through. Now would be the time to add your meat. Mix gravy according to package and add to pot. Add tomato paste, vinegar and sugar to taste…. Bon appetite!

MEATLOAF WITH AU GRATIN POTATOES

Ingredients:

- ✓ 1 old stale dinner roll (bread crumbs work just as well)
- ✓ 1 bundle of fresh parsley
- ✓ 1 Egg
- ✓ 1 small onion, chopped
- ✓ 1 ½ lb. mixture of ground beef and ground pork
- ✓ ½ tablespoon mustard
- ✓ Salt, pepper, nutmeg to taste (garlic powder is optional)
- ✓ ¼ lb. block of Gouda cheese
- ✓ 1 teaspoon French herb seasoning
- ✓ 2 lbs. potatoes
- ✓ ½ to 1 pint half and half

In a large bowl, mix the breadcrumbs (if using stale dinner roll, water it then squeeze out the water). Wash and chop parsley and chopped onion. Add pork/beef mix along with egg and mustard. Mix all ingredients well. Form meat mixture in the center of a flat oversized baking dish. Cut Gouda cheese into sticks and place in the center of the meat mixture. Sprinkle the seasonings onto the top of the cheese. Pull up side and shape into a meatloaf.

Clean, peel and slice potatoes and layer around the meatloaf. Season potatoes with the salt, pepper, and nutmeg. Pour your half and on and around the potatoes. Bake in a 350 degrees oven for one hour, or until meat is cooked through. Barbara likes to serve this dish with peas with mushrooms and pearl onions.

MUSCA CHOLI & MEATBALLS

Meatballs
- 2-3 lbs. ground beef
- 2 eggs
- 2 cups Italian breadcrumbs
- 1 tablespoon water
- Salt and pepper

Mix the above ingredients and shape into balls about 1 to 2 inches in size.

Sauce
- 3- 12oz. cans of tomato paste
- 1 cup sugar
- 2 tablespoons salt
- 1 tablespoon oregano
- 1 tablespoon basil
- 3 tablespoons onion flakes
- 1 tablespoon garlic powder
- 4 cans water (use paste cans)
- 16 oz. pkg. of mostaccioli pasta, cooked and drained.

Put all ingredients into crockpot and cook on high for 3-4 hours, stirring often.

Feeds several hungry people. Goes well with a tossed salad and garlic bread!

One final recipe from my sis, Cindy is listed below! I am not sure I have tasted it, but will do now after reading it!

NANA'S CHICKEN CACCIATORE

- ¼ cup olive oil
- 1 teaspoon basil
- 3 lbs. cut up chicken 1 teaspoon oregano
- 2 med. onions, chopped
- ½ teaspoon celery seed
- 1 can (16oz) Italian tomatoes
- bay leaf
- 1 8 oz. can tomato sauce
- Salt & pepper
- 2 cloves garlic, chopped

Brown chicken in olive oil. Remove chicken and cook onions and garlic until onions are tender, but not browned. Combine remaining ingredients. Return chicken and add tomatoes and tomato sauce. Simmer for about 45 minutes.

Serves well over spaghetti noodles or pasta of your choice.

The Gathering Table

REUBEN CASSEROLE

- ✓ 6 slices of rye bread, cubed
- ✓ 16 oz. can of sauerkraut, drained and rinsed (if desired)
- ✓ 1 lb. sliced corned beef, cut into strips
- ✓ ¾ cup Thousand Island dressing
- ✓ 2 cups shredded Swiss cheese

Arrange bread cubes in a 13x9 baking pan; cover with sauerkraut. Layer corned beef over sauerkraut; drizzle salad dressing over the top. Cover with foil and bake at 400 degrees for 20 minutes. Remove foil; sprinkle with cheese and bake uncovered for another 10 minutes or until cheese is melted and bubbly. This recipe will serve 6 hearty helpings! Enjoy!

SALMON SPAGHETTI WITH CREAM SAUCE

- ½ to 2/3 lb. spaghetti, cooked
- 1½ lb. fresh salmon
- 4 shallots, or 1 bunch green onions
- 1 pt. white wine (Moscato)
- 1 qt. heavy whipping cream
- ½ lb. English peas (frozen)
- Dill Salt & pepper
- Lemon juice
- Parm. cheese, shredded
- 1 tablespoon olive oil Parsley & fresh minced Garlic

Boil Spaghetti in water, drain. Cook salmon in deep skillet with onions be sure not to overcook your salmon!. Add wine. Pour in cream. Season with dill, salt and pepper and lemon Juice. Add peas (These can be optional if preferred.). Finally, thicken with the Parm cheese, and if preferred, add the parsley and freshly minced garlic. Serve salmon and sauce over the spaghetti. This will bring your taste buds alive!

SICILIAN MEAT ROLL (MEATLOAF)

- ✓ 2 eggs
- ✓ ½ cup tomato juice
- ✓ ¼ teaspoon salt
- ✓ ¾ teaspoon oregano
- ✓ 2 garlic cloves, minced
- ✓ ¼ teaspoon pepper
- ✓ 2 lbs. ground beef
- ✓ ¾ cup soft bread crumbs
- ✓ 2 tablespoon parsley
- ✓ 8 thin slices fully cooked ham
- ✓ 1 ½ cups shredded mozzarella
- ✓ 3 thin slices of mozzarella

In a large bowl, combine eggs, juice, and seasonings. Add bread crumbs and beef. Mix thoroughly. On a piece of aluminum foil, pat meat mixture into a 12x10 rectangle. Place ham and shredded cheese on meat to within 1 inch of edges. Roll up jelly-roll style and seal ends and edge. Begin peeling away from foil from the short end as you go. Place seam side down on a greased baking sheet. Bake at 350 degrees for 1 hour and 10 minutes. Top with cheese slices. And bake another 5 minutes for cheese to melt. Remove from oven. This will serve approx. eight people. (Note: she noted that if her husband ate it, then it would only serve two!)

This is Emily and her son Mason at Peoria Zoo! We are all kids at heart even as we grow into our adult selves. Another life lesson from my mom…never lose the child within us!

SHRIMP ETOUFFEE

- ✓ 1 lb. shrimp, raw and shelled
- ✓ 1 bunch green onions (6 to 8), chopped
- ✓ 3 tablespoons grated fresh parsley
- ✓ ½ cup bell pepper, chopped
- ✓ 1 stick butter
- ✓ 2 cans cream of mushroom soup
- ✓ 1 can Rotel tomatoes
- ✓ 3 tablespoons Tony's Seasoning (usually found near meat dept.)
- ✓ 1 teaspoon red pepper
- ✓ 2 teaspoons fresh chopped garlic
- ✓ ½ teaspoon salt

Take shrimp in a bowl and season with Tony's seasoning, red pepper, garlic, salt, and parsley. Set aside. Melt butter and saute onion and bell pepper. Add Rotel tomatoes. Add seasoned shrimp and stir until shrimp is cooked. Add the cream of mushroom soup and stir until smooth. This is great served over a bed of rice. Total time is approx. 30 minutes. **I have a habit of usually adding additional items as I see fit. Perhaps a stalked of chopped celery and some fresh mushrooms. Also, if cream of mushroom soup is not to your liking, you can substitute the cream of chicken as well. (I would also put in some diced chicken as well to make it even heartier!)

Another favorite dish we've had during our visits is Catfish Coubion (Coo-bee-yon).

The Gathering Table

TACO'S

(Back in the early 60's, we did not have hard taco shells, so this is Mom's Recipe—which I think has made its way back!)

- ✓ Soft corn tortillas 4-5 per person (approx. 50)
- ✓ 1.5 to 2 lbs. ground beef
- ✓ 2 cups hand shredded cheddar cheese (more if desired)
- ✓ Finely chopped lettuce
- ✓ Finely chopped tomatoes

Brown ground beef, add salt and pepper if desired and chop into smaller chunks. Remove from skillet and let drain on paper towels.

In an iron skillet, add a small amount of oil and cook each side of the tortilla to a soft pliable. Once removed from skillet, add meat and cheese then use a toothpick and pick top sides together and set in a baking pan/cookie sheet, etc. Once all are finished put in the oven and bake for approx. 8-10 minutes to get the cheese melted. Remove then when getting ready to serve, remove toothpick, add your lettuce, tomato and if prefer, salsa. (we had home canned) Recipe to follow. And take that first crunchy bite… best original taco I have ever had! Of course, hot sauce is a favorite on top as well. I will guarantee all be gone in one sitting.

Additional info: If you like refried beans, they go great on these as well!

(Note: you can reduce the amount of ingredients depending how many you are serving)

Kathy Mitrano

TAMALE PIE

Crust
- 1 box Jiffy corn muffin mix
- 1 egg
- ½ cup sour cream

Mix well and put in a cast iron skillet and bake for 400 in a pre-heated oven for 20 minutes. Remove from oven and poke holes in the corn cake.

Sauce
- 1/3 cup enchilada sauce
- 1 onion, chopped
- 2 tablespoons garlic powder
- 1 teaspoon cumin
- 1 teaspoon chili powder

Mix the above ingredients well and pour over and in the holes of the crust.

Topping
- 1-2 lbs. cooked and drained ground beef**
- 1 cup shredded cheddar cheese
- 1 cup Monterey Jack cheese

**I am sure cooked sausage would be just as good!

Top the crust with the layer of the cheese and cooked meat. Cover with foil and bake in the oven for an additional 20 minutes at 350 degrees. Remove foil carefully so as not to get steam burns! (my personal hint: spray foil with Pam, so the cheese does not stick to foil when removing! Dig in and Enjoy!

Another recipe from Cindy, she is indeed a great cook and queen of her kitchen as well!

TORTELLINI SOUP WITH SAUSAGE AND SPINACH

- ✓ 1 lb. ground pork sausage
- ✓ 1 tablespoon vegetable oil
- ✓ ¾ cup diced onion1 tablespoon minced onion
- ✓ ½ cup fresh sliced mushrooms
- ✓ ½ cup chopped celery
- ✓ 1 large can diced tomatoes (I used my home canned tomatoes!)
- ✓ 1 32oz. box of broth (chicken, vegetable, or even beef)
- ✓ 2 tablespoons chopped basil
- ✓ 1 tablespoon Italian seasoning
- ✓ 1 teaspoon salt
- ✓ ½ teaspoon pepper
- ✓ 1 pkg. refrigerated tortellini
- ✓ 2 cups fresh spinach

In large pan, heat oil and saute onion, celery, and mushrooms. Crumble the sausage and garlic into the vegetable mix. Cook until sausage is no longer pink.

Drain any standing grease from sausage. Stir in tomatoes, broth, salt, and pepper. Reduce heat to low and let simmer for 20 to 30 minutes. Add tortellini and spinach and simmer another 10 minutes or until pasta is tender. Fresh shredded Parmesan cheese is a great topper for this. I sometimes make a double batch, and it all gets eaten!

My Sister-in-Law, Barb came over to the US from Germany and with her, brought some of her Granny's recipes. She had to translate them from the German language into English. I have spent much time visiting her in Louisiana, and she will usually try out a German recipe on me.

Vegetables and Side Dishes

BUTTERNUT SQUASH CASSEROLE

- ✓ 1 medium butternut squash
- ✓ 2 tablespoons butter, melted
- ✓ 2 tablespoons light brown sugar
- ✓ ½ teaspoon salt
- ✓ ¼ teaspoon ground nutmeg
- ✓ ¼ teaspoon ground allspice
- ✓ pinch of ground black pepper

Cut the squash into quarters, remove seeds and skin. *(Butternut squash is a very hard-shell squash. I find it helpful to slice it into 2-inch slices, and it becomes easier to remove the skin.)*

Once the seeds and skin are removed, chop into 1" cubes. Put the squash on a steamer rack in a large saucepan over boiling water and cover. Steam for 30 minutes or until tender. (If no steamer is available, just boil in water enough to cover squash until tender). When it becomes tender, drain and use a potato masher and mash until smooth. Add remaining ingredients and continue mashing until everything is mixed well. Let rest for at least 10 minutes for flavors to mingle. You may reheat in the microwave for a minute or so before serving. We now use butternut squash at Thanksgiving in place of the potatoes. Great flavor. Worth the try!

Kathy Mitrano

BUTTERNUT SQUASH MAC & CHEESE

- 12 oz. dried rigatoni
- 1½ lbs. squash, peeled, seeded and cut into chunks (3 ½ cups)
- 2 ¾ cups milk
- ¼ cup flour
- 8 oz. Gruyere cheese, shredded
- 8 slices bacon
- 2 sweet onions, chunked
- 3 oz. sourdough bread
- 2 tablespoons butter
- Fresh flat leaf parsley

Preheat oven to 425 degrees. Lightly butter a 3-qt. baking dish; set aside. Cook pasta according to directions. Drain and transfer to a large bowl. In a large saucepan combine squash and 2 ½ cups of the milk over med. high heat. Bring to boil, then simmer and cook until squash is tender. (18-20min) Mix together the remaining milk and flour and put into squash and again, bring to a boil until thickened. Stir in the Gruyere until melted. Keep warm.

In a skillet, cook bacon until crisp, drain on paper towel, keeping 2 T of bacon drippings. Crumble, then set aside. In the drippings, add onions and cook and stir until golden.

Add squash mixture, onions and bacon to the bowl of pasta. Toss well to combine, then transfer to baking dish. In a food processor, pulse the bread until it is coarse crumbs. (about 2 cups) Mix together the crumbs and melted butter. Sprinkle remaining cheese and crumb mix over the top of pasta. Bake until top is browned (15 minutes). Cool 5 minutes sprinkle with parsley. 6-8 servings. Enjoy!

NOTE: This is an excellent recipe. Living in a smaller community, our local stores do not have a large variety of cheeses. I did find Gruyere at a larger grocery store, but if I could not, I did look for what a good substitute would be. This cheese is somewhat like Swiss, only stronger. Also, havarti can be substituted. You would like to have a nuttier tasting cheese for this dish. I did include photos as I was making this!

The Gathering Table

CAULIFLOWER IN CHEESE SAUCE

- 1 large head cauliflower
- 2 egg yolks
- Salt to taste
- ¼ teaspoon paprika
- ½ lb. provolone or Muenster
- 1 tablespoon butter
- 1 pkg. white gravy mix
- 1 tablespoon breadcrumbs
- ½ cup cream
- ½ cup reserved water from
- cauliflower

Clean cauliflower and quarter and soak in salt water about 10 minutes. Bring 2 cup salt water to boil. Add cauliflower. Meanwhile, mix together gravy mix, egg yolk, paprika, and cream. Lower heat and cover to simmer for 25 minutes. Drain and dry cauliflower. Place in casserole dish, pour shredded cheese over the top. Top that with bread crumbs and finally the butter. Broil dish in a 375 degree until cheese is golden brown. **Note: she had to convert the measurements, but had those right. If needed season less or more to taste! (Serves approx. 4).

CREOLE FRIED RICE

**Note: This recipe works best with cold rice. If possible, make the rice a day before and store in the fridge. If unable to do this, when you make the rice, when done, spread on a cookie sheet to cool completely

- ✓ 1 cup uncooked long grain rice
- ✓ 2 cups chicken broth
- ✓ 1 lb. chicken thigh skinned and boned
- ✓ 1 ½ teaspoons Creole seasoning mix,
- ✓ 2 tablespoons vegetable oil
- ✓ ½ lb. andouille or smoked sausage, sliced
- ✓ ½ small onion, chopped
- ✓ ½ green pepper, chopped
- ✓ 2 garlic cloves, chopped
- ✓ 1 cup fresh sliced okra,
- ✓ 3 plum tomatoes, chopped
- ✓ 2 green onions, sliced

Cook rice according to package directions, substituting chicken broth for the water. (If cooking the rice the same day, spread on a cooking sheet and let cool for no less than 30 minutes; longer if needed.) Cut chicken thighs into 1-inch pieces and toss with 1 teaspoon of creole seasoning. Heat oil in large skillet and over medium heat cook chicken, add sausage and cook 3-4 minutes or until lightly browned. Add onions, peppers, and garlic Cook 5 minutes or until onions are done and translucent. Stir in okra and remaining seasoning. Increase heat to high and add rice and cook stirring constantly for 4 minutes or until thoroughly heated. Sprinkle with sliced green onions and serve immediately.

FRIED CORN

- 5-6 ears of fresh corn, removed from cob
- 2 tablespoons sugar
- 1 ½ teaspoons salt
- 2 tablespoons flour
- 1 ¼ cups water
- 3 slices bacon, fried crisp, and crumbled (reserve some of the grease)

Once corn is removed from cob, mix sugar, salt, flour, and water. Add corn and place in a skillet with bacon grease. Cook about 20 minutes, stirring often. Before serving, add crumbled bacon over the top.

LAYERED SPAGHETTI SQUASH

- ✓ 1 medium spaghetti squash (about 3 lbs.)
- ✓ 1 lb. pork sausage
- ✓ 1 medium onion, chopped
- ✓ 3 garlic cloves, chopped
- ✓ 2 teaspoon Italian seasoning (divided)
- ✓ 15 oz. ricotta cheese
- ✓ 1 teaspoon garlic powder
- ✓ 1 teaspoon parsley
- ✓ 1 tablespoon Parmesan cheese
- ✓ salt & pepper
- ✓ Jar of favorite red sauce
- ✓ 1 pkg. mozzarella cheese, shredded.

Preheat oven to 375 degrees. Cut squash in half lengthwise and place face down on a baking sheet with about ¼ inch of water. Bake for about 30 minutes, or until you can pierce the squash, about six times. Out of the oven in another dish, place squash in microwave on high for about 10 minutes. Remove and let cool. While the squash is cooking, cook the sausage, breaking the meat apart as cooking. Add the seasoning, chopped onion and garlic, saute until fully cooked.

Open ricotta and add 1 teaspoon of seasoning, garlic powder, parm cheese, salt, and pepper. Mix well and set aside.

Back to the squash: Carefully with a spoon, scoop out the seeds and discard. With a fork, scrape out the squash "noodles" placing them in a separate bowl. Keep scraping until all squash is removed, preserving the "shell" as that will be what you bake in. Layers: Equally, put a layer of noodles in the bottom of the shell*, top with your sauce. Add a layer of ricotta, sausage and another layer of squash, sauce, and sausage. Top all that with the shredded cheese. Using equal amounts to fill both halves of shells. Bake in the oven for about 35 min. You can slice this out through shell for ease. This pairs well with a salad on the side!

*IF you do not want to use the shells, feel free to use a small baking dish and make your layers it that. It all works well either way!

Kathy Mitrano

ONION SHORTCAKE

- 2 large onions, thinly sliced.
- 1 stick of butter
- 8 oz. sour cream
- ½ teaspoon dill weed
- ¼ teaspoon salt
- 8 oz. cheddar cheese, divided
- 15 oz. can creamed corn
- ½ cup milk
- 8 ½ oz. pkg. Jiffy muffin mix
- 1 egg, slightly beaten
- 4 drops of hot pepper sauce

Saute onions in butter. Stir in sour cream, dill weed, salt and ½ of the cheddar cheese

Combine corn, milk, dry muffin mix, egg and hot pepper drops.

Put corn mixture into a buttered 9x13 baking dish (sprayed with Pam or grease).

Spread onion mixture over the top and top that with the remaining cheese.

Bake at 375 for approx. 20 minutes. Remove from oven and serve.

The Gathering Table

SMOTHERED GREENS

- 3 cups water
- ¼ lb. smoked turkey breast
- 1 tablespoon hot pepper
- ¼ teaspoon cayenne pepper
- ¼ teaspoon ground cloves
- ½ teaspoon thyme
- 2 cloves garlic, chopped
- 2 scallions, chopped
- 1 teaspoon ginger
- 2 lbs. greens (fresh)

Boil all ingredients, except the greens. Once boiling, add the greens and cook another 20 minutes until cooked through and tender.

Kathy Mitrano

SPECIAL BEANS

- ✓ 1 lb. bacon, chopped
- ✓ 1 medium onion, chopped

Saute both for 5 minutes or until bacon is done. Drain off grease.

Add ½ cup water, and boil 10 minutes. Add ½ cup packed brown sugar Add another ½ cup water and boil another 10 minutes

Add the following:
- ✓ 1 large can Bush beans
- ✓ 14 oz can kidney beans, drained
- ✓ 14-15 oz. can butter beans, drained
- ✓ 14 oz. lima beans, drained

Mix all ingredients together then. Heat and eat!

SPINACH AND RICE SIDE DISH

- ✓ 1 cup uncooked rice**
- ✓ 1 medium onion, chopped
- ✓ ⅓ cup olive oil
- ✓ 2 cups chicken broth
- ✓ 1 ½ teaspoons salt
- ✓ 10 oz. package frozen spinach

Saute rice and onion in olive oil. Add 2 cups boiling chicken stock and salt. Cover and simmer for 10 minutes. Add spinach, (thawed and drained well) and again cover and simmer about 15 minutes or until done and rice is tender.

**Depending on your preference of rice, you may use long grain and wild rice or plain white rice. We love it either way; it just a matter of your own preference. Enjoy! Also, this is a great side dish with baked chicken, or pork chops or roast.

TWICE BAKED POTATOES

- 4 baking potatoes, washed
- 1 ½ tablespoons canola oil
- 1 stick salted butter
- ½ cup bacon bits
- ½ cup sour cream
- ½ cup cheddar and Cojack cheese, plus extra
- ¼ cup whole milk

I usually use ½ & ½ for a creamier filling

- Salt & pepper to taste
- 3 green onions sliced

Preheat oven to 400 degrees. Place potatoes on a baking sheet. Rub with canola oil and bake for about an hour, making sure they are cooked sufficiently through. While the potatoes are baking, if you are using bacon, now is the time to fry this and drain on paper towels. Once cooled crumble into bacon bits. You can use precooked bacon bits if preferred.

Slice your butter into pats. Place in a mixing bowl. Add bacon and sour cream. Remove the potatoes from the oven and lower the heat to 350 degrees.

With a sharp knife, cut each potato in half lengthwise. Scrape the insides into the mixing bowl, being careful not to tear the skins. Leave some potato in the shell just for support. Lay the hollowed shells on a baking sheet.

Smash the potatoes into the butter, bacon, sour cream. Add the ½ cup cheese, milk (or half & half) salt, green onions, and pepper to taste. Mix well.

Fill the shells with the filling. Top each potato with more of the cheese, bacon and additional green onion if desired. Put in oven until warmed through. 15-25 minutes. (I will usually bake my potatoes the night before, to help cut prep time on the day of.) Growing up in a large family, I learned to cook from my mom, so needless to say, I always end up with leftovers! That is not a terrible thing.

Along with a large family, when we all get together, we make large dishes to accommodate all appetites and enough left over to dole out to take home.

The Gathering Table

ZESTY CARROT BAKE

- ✓ 1 lb. carrots, sliced
- ✓ 2 tablespoons minced onion
- ✓ ¾ cup mayonnaise
- ✓ 1/3 cup water
- ✓ 1 tablespoon horseradish
- ✓ Pepper to taste
- ✓ ½ cup breadcrumbs
- ✓ 2 tablespoons butter, melted
- ✓ ½ cup sharp cheddar cheese, shredded

Cook carrots until tender (reserve ⅓ cup of water used). Place carrots in a 1 qt. casserole dish. In a small bowl, combine onion, mayo, water, pepper, and horseradish. Mix well and pour over carrots. Combine melted butter and breadcrumbs mix and sprinkle on top of casserole. Bake in a 350-degree oven for 25-30 minutes. Sprinkle with cheese and return to oven for another 2-3 minutes. Serve and Enjoy!

Tired of the same old cooked carrots? This recipe puts a zest to the flavor. Again, from my sis-in-law. Great alternative to this veggie.

ZUCCHINI-POTATO CASSEROLE

- 2 tablespoons butter
- 2 medium sweet onions,
- 1 medium Yukon Gold potato, sliced
- 1 medium size zucchini, sliced
- 4 plum tomatoes, sliced
- 1½ teaspoons salt
- ¾ teaspoon pepper
- 2 tablespoons butter melted
- ⅓ cup fresh grated Parmesan
- cooking spray

Preheat oven to 375 degrees. Melt 2 tablespoons butter in a medium skillet over medium heat. Add onions and saute 10 to 12 minutes or until onions begin to caramelize. Spoon onions into a 10" baking dish coated with cooking spray. Toss together potatoes and next 4 ingredients. Arrange potatoes, zucchini, and tomatoes in a single layer over onions. Drizzle with remaining 2 tablespoons butter and sprinkle with cheese. Bake 3 to 40 minutes or until golden brown. Let stand 10 min. before serving. Serves 4-6.

BAKED SHRIMP & CRAB SALAD

- 1 bell pepper, chopped
- 1 onion, chopped
- 1 cup celery, chopped fine
- 6 oz. lump crab meat
- 1 bag, small shrimp (cocktail size) tails and shell
- ¾ cup mayo
- salt and pepper to taste
- 1 teaspoon Worcestershire sauce
- 1 cup seasoned breadcrumbs

Combine all the vegetables and seafood. Mix well. Add mayo and seasonings. Put mixture into a buttered casserole dish. Top with the seasoned breadcrumbs. Bake at 350 degrees approx. 30 minutes. Great served with various crackers!

BROCCOLI AND BACON SALAD

- 1 large bunch of fresh broccoli, separated into florets
- 1 small red onion, coarsely chopped
- 1 cup raisins
- 10-12 bacon strips cooked and crumbled (I usually cut my bacon into small pieces, so it's already crumbled when done)

Dressing:
- 2 tablespoons vinegar
- 1/3 cup mayonnaise
- ½ cup sugar

Combine broccoli, red onion, raisins into bowl. Mix dressing ingredients and pour over broccoli mixture. Cover and refrigerate overnight. Great blend of flavors!

The following fruit salad recipe came from a former co-worker. We loved when we had parties at our work! Everyone brought their dishes, then later in the day, the emails were kept hopping from passing recipes back and forth.

CREAMY FRUIT SALAD

(This is a double batch that you can cut in half to accommodate your crowd or increase as needed! Enjoy the refreshing flavors!)

- ✓ 2 3 oz. boxes of Orange Jell-O
- ✓ 2 12 oz. Cool Whip
- ✓ 2 11 oz. cans mandarin oranges, drained
- ✓ 2 15 oz. cans crushed pineapple with juice
- ✓ 1 cup pecans (Optional)
- ✓ 2 cups mini marshmallows

In a large bowl, stir Jell-O into cool whip until smooth. Add drained oranges.

Add pineapple with juices. Add marshmallows and nuts. Stir all very well and cover. Refrigerate until ready to serve.

**This is a great dish for those watching weight or diabetic; you can get these ingredients sugar free.

DEE'S CABBAGE SLAW

- 1 head cabbage, shredded
- ½ -1 cup raisins
- ¾ cup chopped red onion
- 1 apple, sliced, (peel if desired)
- ¼ cup mayonnaise.

Mix all ingredients well and adjust as needed (i.e., increase mayo or if needed add a small amount of sugar).

The Gathering Table

FRESH BROCCOLI SALAD

- 1 medium bunch broccoli
- (cleaned and chopped)
- 1 can kidney beans, drained
- 1 small red onion, chopped fine
- 1 pkg. Good Seasons Italian Dressing Mix
- 1 cup grated sharp cheddar cheese

Prepare dressing according to package directions. Mix all other ingredients in a large bowl. Cover tightly and refrigerate overnight. Serves 8-10.

ITALIAN RESTAURANT SALAD

- ✓ 1 head iceberg lettuce
- ✓ 2 cups spring mix
- ✓ ¼ cup white onion, thinly sliced
- ✓ ½ cup artichoke hearts, diced
- ✓ 1 red pepper, diced
- ✓ ½ cup fresh Parmesan grated

Dressing

- ✓ ¼ cup red wine vinegar
- ✓ 1 teaspoon garlic salt
- ✓ 1 teaspoon cracked pepper
- ✓ 1 teaspoon dried Italian seasons
- ✓ 1 tablespoon sugar, honey or Karo syrup
- ✓ herbs
- ✓ ¼ cup olive oil

Wash greens and let drain or spin dry. Add onion, artichoke hearts and peppers to lettuce in a large bowl. Refrigerate. For the dressing: whisk together all but the olive oil. Slowly whisk in olive oil. Shake well before tossing with salad. Top with Parm. cheese and serve cold.

MACARONI SALAD

- 5 cups macaroni, cooked, drained & cooled
- 1 cup celery, chopped
- 1 cup broccoli, chopped
- 1 cup green pepper, chopped
- 1 cup carrots, shredded
- 1 cup onion, chopped (purple or white)
- 1 block cheddar cheese in small cubes

Sauce
- 3 cups Miracle Whip
- ⅔ cup sugar
- ¾ cup milk
- ¾ cup French dressing (Catalina) (homemade recipe to follow)
- Mix all ingredients and chill for 2 hours.

French dressing**
- ⅔ cup catsup
- ½ cup sugar
- ½ cup vinegar
- ½ cup oil

Mix very well and use in place of the Catalina dressing.

This makes a large amount to feed all your hungry guests with enough left over to snack on later! ** The French dressing recipe can be used in place of sauce.

MATT'S YEARLY BIRTHDAY DINNER!

On his birthday, my son, Matthew gets a meal of his choosing cooked by none other than….Mom! He persuaded me several years ago to make a lamb dinner. I had never cooked lamb before so needless to say, I was somewhat apprehensive as to what I was doing. I did my reading and web browsing and talking with the butcher at the store. I felt I was up to the task and the butcher was kind enough to mix up a seasoning for me to use. I am now making at least one lamb dinner a year and the only thing that changes each year is his birthday cake. His meal consists of the boneless leg of lamb, garlic cheese bombs, Strawberry Arugula Salad, twice baked potatoes, (have also done garlic mashed potatoes as well).

STRAWBERRY ARUGULA SPRING SALAD

- ✓ 6 cups (5-8oz) loosely packed baby arugula
- ✓ 2 cups strawberries, sliced

Dressing:
- ✓ 3 tablespoons grapeseed oil
- ✓ 2 tablespoons white wine vinegar
- ✓ 2 tablespoons sugar
- ✓ 1 tablespoon chopped onion
- ✓ 1 tablespoon sesame seed

- ✓ 1 small sweet onion, thinly sliced
- ✓ ½ cup toasted pecans

- ✓ ½ teaspoon Worcestershire sauce
- ✓ ¼ teaspoon smoked paprika
- ✓ ¼ teaspoon kosher salt
- ✓ ½ cup goat cheese, crumbled (optional)

In a small skillet, toast the pecans if using over medium heat tossing frequently until fragrant (approx. 2 minutes). Place the pecans in a small dish and set aside.

In a large salad bowl, combine arugula, strawberries and sliced onion. For the dressing: In a blender or processor, combine the oil, vinegar, sugar, sesame seeds, chopped onion, Worcestershire sauce, paprika, and salt. Blend until all ingredients are pureed. Taste and you may adjust accordingly (more sugar, etc.).

**I get this made ahead of time and refrigerate and do not put on salad until ready to eat. You may be sparing with it, and each guest can add to their likeness. Toss the blended vinaigrette into salad bowl ingredients. Garnish tops with toasted pecans and goat cheese once each guest has on their salad plate.

Kathy Mitrano

PAM'S PASTA SALAD

Dressing mix:
- 1½ cups sugar
- 1½ teaspoons pepper
- 1½ cups water
- 2 tablespoons mustard
- 1 cup oil
- 1 teaspoon parsley
- 1 teaspoon salt
- 1 teaspoon dill weed
- 1 teaspoon garlic powder (I use 1 clove minced garlic)

Mix together the dressing ingredients until well blended

Salad ingredients:
- 1 green pepper, seeded and chopped
- 1 yellow pepper, seeded and chopped
- 1 red pepper, seeded and chopped
- Green onions washed and sliced (as many to your liking)
- Peels and sliced cucumbers (English cucumbers are a perfect size)
- 16 oz. box Pasta, boiled, drained and cooled. (Again, your choice of pasta)

Boil pasta according to directions and when done, drain and cool slightly. Add all your chopped vegetables and be sure to give your refrigerated dressing mix a good shake or two and pour onto salad. Mix well. Cover and refrigerate until ready to serve. This is a beautifully colorful dish to serve at BBQ's!

Pam's oldest child, Charlie, is again no stranger to the Kitchen. As I had stated, cooking genes have been passed on to our children as well! Charlie loves to cook!

This is a recipe he loves to make. I am not even sure where it came from or if it was part of a thinking process!

RICE ARTICHOKE SALAD

- 1 pkg. chicken Rice-a-Roni
- 2 heads broccoli,
- 2 green onions, chopped
- 1 bell pepper, any color
- 1 small can black olives, drained
- 1-6oz jar marinated artichokes, if desired reserve liquid for dressing

**1-2 cups cubed chicken,

Dressing

- ½ teaspoon curry
- ⅓ cup mayonnaise
- Marinade from artichokes

Cook rice according to the package. Allow to cool. Clean broccoli and cut into bite-size pieces. Add remaining ingredients and mix well. Add dressing, stir well. Refrigerate until dinner time!

I am not a huge fan of kale, but I was given the following recipe from my sister in law, and I believe this is another go to that I love!

SPINACH SALAD

- 2 bags fresh spinach, washed and stemmed
- ½ pound bacon, fried and crumbled
- 1 pkg. Uncle Ben's Long Grain and Wild Rice w/seasonings
- 1-2 stalks celery, diced.

Ingredients:

In a large bowl, put cleaned spinach, being sure to clip the stems off. (Baby Spinach would work well with this). I just made this and added chopped water chestnuts for an added crunch!

Fry the bacon drain and crumble (I normally chop my bacon before frying then drain on paper towel to get excess fat off).

Cook rice according to package directions. Once done, spread on a cookie sheet to cool.

Dressing:

- 1 pkg. Good Seasons Italian dressing mix
- Soy sauce
- 1 teaspoon sugar

Prepare dressing as indicated on the package. (a cruet works great). Shake well to mix. Add soy sauce to about an inch from the top. (you want the dressing to be somewhat dark) ** Low sodium soy is a suitable alternative as well. Add sugar, shake well. If you care, you can play with the measurements to your satisfaction of sweetness.

Combine all ingredients in a salad bowl mix well and refrigerate until ready to serve. This is a good change from slaws and potato salads!

Dessert

The Gathering Table

My grandchildren love being in the kitchen helping with cooking or setting the table for dinner. The following pictures were taken when my granddaughter Kylie, 10 at the time, was making myself and Gramma Debbie desserts. With a little help from me and of course her doing most of the work. They came out great, and you can see by the photos, she was quite proud of her creations!

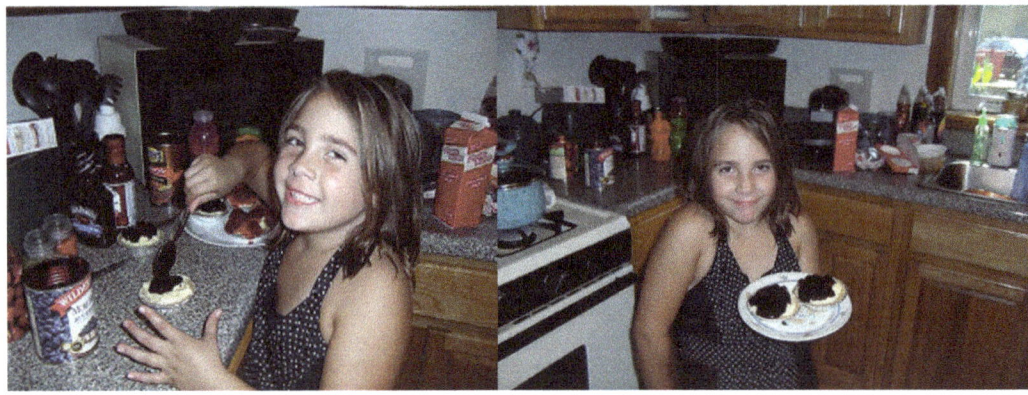

Kylie & I am mixing cheesecake Kylie putting the topping on! Posing with her master creation!

ANGEL LUSH TRIFLE CAKE

- ½ cup sweetened condensed milk
- 1½ cups cold water
- 1 pkg. instant vanilla pudding mix
- 1-8 oz. frozen whipped topping,
- 1 prepared angel food cake thawed
- 4 cups fresh sliced strawberries
- 3-5 whole strawberries

In a bowl, whisk the milk and water. Whisk in the pudding mix and whisk another 2 minutes. Let stand for 2 minutes, or until soft set. Fold in the whipped topping. Cut the angel food cake into ½ inch cubes. Spoon a third of the pudding mixture into a 4-qt. trifle or glass bowl. Top with half of the cake cubes and sliced strawberries. Repeat layers once. Top with remaining pudding mixture and garnish with the whole strawberries on the top. Keep refrigerated until ready to eat.

**Note: I will sometimes add either well-drained pineapple, crushed or cubes for added flavor.

The Gathering Table

APPLE BETTY

- 6 cups sliced apples (approx. 2 lbs.)
- 1 lemon, grated peel, and juice
- ⅓ cup brown sugar
- ⅓ cup sugar
- 1 teaspoon cinnamon
- ½ teaspoon cardamom
- 2 cups soft bread crumbs
- ¼ cup melted butter

In a large bowl, combine apples, lemon peel, and juice, sugars, cinnamon, and cardamom. Toss to coat apples with flavorings. Begin layering in a 2-qt. baking dish with bread crumbs, alternating with apple mixture. Top off with crumbs. Pour melted butter over the top. Cook on high in the microwave for 8 to 10 minutes or until apples are tender. Serve with cream or Vanilla ice cream if desired. Serves 6 to 8.

APPLE CRISP

- 4 cups sliced pared tart apples (about 4-5 medium)
- ⅔ to ¾ cup brown sugar, packed
- ½ cup all-purpose flour
- ½ cup uncooked rolled oats
- ¾ teaspoon cinnamon
- ¾ teaspoon nutmeg
- ⅓ cup butter, softened

Heat oven to 375 degrees. Grease square pan (8x8). Spread apple slices in pan. Mix remaining ingredients thoroughly and sprinkle over apples. Bake until apples are tender, and topping is golden brown. About 30 minutes. Serve warm and if desired, with light cream or ice cream. This will make approx. 6 servings.

BAKED APPLES

- 4 baking apples (Rome Beauty, Pippin or Granny Smith)
- Lemon juice
- ¼ cup brown sugar
- ¼ cup raisins
- ¼ cup slivered almonds
- 1 teaspoon cinnamon
- 4 teaspoons butter

Core apples. Peel skin from the top half of each apple. Arrange apples in a round baking dish (8 in). Sprinkle with lemon juice. Combine sugar, raisins, almonds, and cinnamon. Fill centers of each apple with sugar mixture. Dot each apple with butter. Cook on high for 8-10 minutes in microwave or until apples are tender. Serves 4.

Kathy Mitrano

BANANA SPLIT DESSERT

Crust:
- 2 cups graham cracker crumbs
- 1 stick melted butter

Combine melted butter with the graham cracker crumbs and mix well. Press into an 8x8 baking ungreased baking dish. Do not bake but instead refrigerate for the crust to set up.

Filling:
- 1 stick butter
- 2 eggs
- 2 cups powdered sugar

Beat the butter, eggs and powdered sugar together in a mixing bowl for about 10 minutes or until well blended. ***NOTE: I have done research on raw eggs in desserts, and they are fine to use if your dessert is a refrigerated dessert.

Spread this layer over the top of the crust that you have refrigerated.

Topping:
- 1 large can crushed pineapple, juice drained as well as possible
- 5 bananas sliced and lay over the top of the pineapple layer
- 1 large container whipped topping thawed, spread over your layer of pineapple
- 1 jar maraschino cherries, drained and stems removed.

Lay the cherries on the top of the whipped topping and sprinkle with nuts. Refrigerate until ready to serve

**Nuts are optional or use your favorite (walnuts, pecans, etc.)

This dish never has any left over by the end of our gathering. Very rich in flavor!

** Also for the size of our family get-togethers, Pam often doubles the recipe into a regular 9x13 cake pan!

BETTER THAN ANYTHING CARAMEL CAKE

- ✓ 1 chocolate cake mix
- ✓ 1-16 oz. jar caramel sauce
- ✓ 1 can sweetened condensed milk
- ✓ 1½ cups heavy whipping cream
- ✓ ¼ cup powdered sugar
- ✓ 1 bag Heath Bar Brickle*

Bake cake according to directions in a 9x13 greased baking pan. Remove cake from oven and let cool about 5 minutes, then using the handle of a long wooden spoon, poke holes in the cake. (I do about 12-14) Immediately pour the caramel sauce over the entire cake. Most will seep into the holes. Next, pour the sweetened condensed milk in the same fashion over the cake. Allow the cake to cool completely. (Can refrigerate while making frosting if desired).

While the cake is cooling, to make the frosting add the heavy whipping cream to a mixing bowl and beat until soft peaks form. Add the powdered sugar and again, beat until stiff peaks form. (Note: you may add a little vanilla if desired, I did not, and it still tasted great!) Smooth the whipped frosting over the entire cake and top with the Health Bar Brickle. A half bag covers the cake well, but use your own judgment! ** Heath Bar Brickle can be found in the baking section near the chocolate chips. Refrigerate until ready to serve. It can also be made the day ahead of time.

Kathy Mitrano

The Gathering Table

BETTER THAN SEX CAKE

- ✓ 1 pkg. butter pudding cake mix
- ✓ 1 large can crushed pineapple
- ✓ 1 cup sugar
- ✓ 1 box instant vanilla pudding
- ✓ 1 carton of Cool Whip
- ✓ 1 can of angel flake coconut
- ✓ Maraschino cherries and chopped pecans

Bake cake according to instructions on the package. Boil pineapple and sugar until all the sugar is dissolved. Pour over warm cake, then let it cool. Mix pudding as directed and pour over cooled cake. Let set. Spread Cool Whip over top of cake, then sprinkle with cherries and nuts. Refrigerate until ready to serve. (the more juice in the pineapple, the better the cake tastes… according to Miss Mary!)

CHOCOLATE OVERLOAD PEANUT BUTTER CAKE

- 1 box chocolate cake mix
- 1 bag of miniature peanut butter cups (Reese's)
- Unwrapped and coarsely chopped (approx..30-40 pcs.)

Follow directions on the cake box for the round pans. Bake according to times indicated. NOTE: I made this into a 3-layer cake by just slicing one of the cakes in half. When removing from oven, carefully turn them out onto wire cooling racks to cool completely.

PEANUT BUTTER FROSTING

- 2 cups confectioners' sugar
- 2 cups creamy peanut butter
- 10 tablespoons softened butter
- 1 ½ teaspoons vanilla extract
- ½ teaspoon salt
- ⅔ cup heavy cream

Place confectioners' sugar, peanut butter, butter, vanilla and salt in a bowl. Mix on medium to medium-low speed until creamy. Scrape down the sides of the bowl with rubber spatula as needed. Add the heavy cream and beat on high speed until the mixture is light and smooth. Set aside for now.

CHOCOLATE GANACHE'

- 8 oz. semi-sweet chocolate, finely chopped
- ¾ cup heavy cream

While the cake is chilling, make the ganache'. Place the chocolate in a 4-cup measuring cup and set aside. Place the cream in a small saucepan over medium to medium-low heat and warm just until It comes to a low boil. Pour the cream over the chocolate and let sit for 2 minutes. Whisk until the ganache' is smooth. Set aside to cool, occasionally whisking, until it has thickened slightly, yet keeping a pouring consistency.

Place one cake layer on serving plate. Cover with 1 cup of the peanut butter frosting and sprinkle with about 10 chopped peanut butter cups. Top with the second layer of cake and frost and sprinkle another 10 chopped peanut butter cups. Place the final layer on top, face down. Frost the cake with remaining frosting top and sides, smoothing as best as possible. Refrigerate the cake for at least 1 hour until the icing is set. Slowly pour the ganache' over the top of the cake, letting it flow over the sides of the cake as well. Top with remaining 10 chopped peanut butter cups. Refrigerate the cake for at least 30 minutes, allowing the ganache' to set up. Keep cake refrigerated and remove 30 minutes prior to serving. Will serve from 12 to 20!

> NOTE: Matt found this recipe and said this is the cake he wanted and sent me the recipe. This is the first time ever that I had worked with making Ganache' and was a little nervous, but turned out ok for the first time!

**This was my very first attempt at working with ganache' and I felt quite intimidated by it, but the taste was spectacular. The lesson is you MUST learn by doing! BTW, I insisted Matt take the cake home; it was HUGE!

Kathy Mitrano

CHOCOLATE CAVITY MAKER CAKE

- ✓ 16 oz. sour cream
- ✓ 3 eggs
- ✓ ⅓ cup vegetable oil
- ✓ ½ strong instant coffee
- ✓ 18.5 oz. dark chocolate cake mix (2 tablespoons granules in ½ cup water)
- ✓ (she uses Duncan Hines dark chocolate fudge cake mix)
- ✓ 3.9 oz. pkg. instant choc. pudding mix
- ✓ 2 cups semi-sweet choc. chips
- ✓ 1 can of chocolate frosting mix.

1. Grease a 10-inch Bundt pan with Crisco or any shortening. If your pan is smaller, you may want to fill it up to about an inch below the rim, then put the extra batter in a smaller cake pan.
2. In a large brown combine the first 4 "wet" ingredients. Mix in the cake mix and instant pudding. Beat for 2 minutes on medium speed.
3. Stir in chocolate chips. Batter will be thick.
4. Spoon into Bundt pan.
5. Bake in a preheated 340 degree oven for 1 hour. Or until done knife insert comes out clean.
6. Remove from oven and let set in pan for 10 minutes. When removing place a large plate over the top and turn upside down. Cool on plate at least an hour before frosting.
7. When cake is completely cooled, apply the can of frosting. If desired you may sprinkle "pretties" on it right away before the icing sets and dries!

**Special note: This cake is much better the next day and each day to come! It may be too soft on the first day. Great to make a day ahead for best results.

Serves 12 (1/12 slice is 536 calories, WITHOUT frosting!) but with a cake as good as this… who is counting!

Cindy also picked up my mom's love of sewing. She has made many quilts. The picture below is a wall hanging or lap quilt she made for all her siblings after my mom passed. We were all so grateful for this as a memory of our family!

From left to right is Pam (oldest sister), Judy, myself and Janet at Christmas. The quilt is a family tree wall quilt she had made for each sibling in honor of our parents passed. This photo was taken in December of 2013.

Kathy Mitrano

CHOCOLATE COVERED CHERRY COOKIES

Ingredients:

- 1½ cups all-purpose flour
- ½ cup unsweetened cocoa powder
- ¼ teaspoon salt
- ¼ teaspoon baking soda
- ¼ teaspoon baking powder
- ½ cup butter (room temp)
- 1 cup granulated sugar
- 1 egg
- 1½ teaspoons vanilla
- 1-10 oz. jar maraschino cherries, drained, reserving juice, and remove stems if attached.
- 1-6 oz. pkg. semi-sweet chocolate chips
- ½ cup sweetened condensed milk

Preparation:

In a large bowl, combine flour, cocoa powder, salt, baking powder and soda, blending well; set aside. In another bowl, beat together butter and sugar on low speed until fluffy. Add egg and vanilla, beat well. Gradually add dry ingredients to the creamed mixture and beat until smooth and well blended. With hands, shape dough into 1" balls and place on UNGREASED baking sheet. Press down the center of each dough ball with your thumb. Place cherry (well drained) in the center of each cookie.

In a small saucepan, combine chocolate chips and sweetened condensed milk until chocolate is melted. Stir in 1 tablespoon plus 1 teaspoon of reserved cherry juice. Spoon about a teaspoon of the chocolate topping over each cherry, spreading to cover the cherry. **If frosting seems too thick, you can thin it by adding small amounts of cherry juice. Bake at 350 degrees for 10 minutes or until done. Remove to wire rack carefully to cool. This should make approx. 3-4 dozen. Completely cool before storing and use wax paper between layers if necessary.

COCONUT CREAM PIE

- 9" pie crust at room temperature (She used Pillsbury pie crust)
- 1 box Jell-O cook and serve vanilla pudding mix (3.4oz)
- 1 box Jell-O cook and serve coconut pudding mix (3.4oz)
- 3 ½ cups whole milk
- 1 tablespoon butter
- ½ teaspoon vanilla
- 1 ¾ cups angel flake coconut, divided
- 1 8 oz. container Cool Whip, thawed

Place room temp. pie crust dough into a 9" pie pan. Roll edges under then crimp with fingers or a fork. Prick pie crust with a fork (keeps it from bubbling up while baking) Bake crust for 10 to 12 minutes. Cool completely before filling.

Combine pudding mixes, milk, butter, vanilla extract and 1 cup of coconut together in a 2 qt. pan. Whisk until well blended. Bring to a hard boil, stirring constantly. Pour into bowl and top with plastic wrap putting the wrap directly onto the pudding. (this keeps the pudding from crusting). Let cool for 30 min. Pour into pie crust. Again, top with plastic wrap. Refrigerate for 3 hours. Top with Cool Whip and toast the remaining coconut. (to toast coconut; place a skillet over medium-high heat and add coconut and constantly stir until lightly browned and toasted, careful not to over toast and burn!)

CRACK CRACKERS

- 35 crackers
- ¾ cup pecans, chopped**
- 1 cup choc. chips
- 1 cup brown sugar
- 1 cup butter

Line cookie sheet with whole crackers. Melt butter, brown sugar and bring to a boil for about 3 minutes. Pour over crackers.

Bake at 375 Degrees oven for 3-5 minutes. Remove from oven and immediately spread chocolate chips directly over crackers. Sprinkle with nuts.

Break into bite-sized pieces. **Chopped walnuts can also be used in place of pecans.

(SOUNDS DELISH TO ME!!!!)

Cindy has as much love for cooking as anyone I know. She can whip up a meal in no time at all, and I can honestly say, I have never had anything even questionably not good!

Through the years of growing up, our mom never made us a stranger to how to cook. We were all fortunate in that respect!

CRANBERRY APPLE CRISP (LOW CAL.)

Filling:
- 3 cups peeled, cored apples
- 2 cups fresh or frozen cranberries (thawed)
- 1 cup Equal sweetener spoonful (24 packets) ***

Topping:
- ⅓ cup all-purpose flour
- ¼ cup chopped pecans
- ¼ cup stick butter, melted
- ½ cup Equal sweetener (12 packets) ***

For filling, combine apples, cranberries, and sweetener in a 10" pie plate. For topping, combine flour, pecans, melted butter and ½ cup equal. Mix until well blended. Sprinkle flour mixture over apples and cranberries in pie plate. Bake in a preheated 350-degree oven for 55 to 60 minutes or until fruit is tender. Serve warm or at room temperature.

***Splenda would also be a good alternative to the Equal. This would also be a great recipe for the diabetic!

Kathy Mitrano

CREAM CHEESE FROSTING

- ✓ 1 8 oz. cream cheese softened
- ✓ 4 tablespoons butter, softened
- ✓ 1 16 oz. box powdered sugar
- ✓ 1 teaspoon vanilla extract
- ✓ ½ cup chopped pecans (for top)

With a mixer, beat cream cheese, butter, vanilla, and sugar until light and fluffy. Spread on the first layer, and top then add the second layer and spread top and sides. Sprinkle the chopped pecans on top.

HUMMINGBIRD CAKE

- Preheat oven to 350 degrees and grease and flour 2 9" round cake pans
- 3 cups all-purpose flour
- 2 cups sugar
- 1 teaspoon each of salt, baking soda, and ground cinnamon
- 1 cup chopped pecans
- In a large bowl, whisk all dry ingredients and set aside.
- 3 eggs
- 1 cup vegetable oil
- 2 teaspoons vanilla extract
- 1 8 oz. can crushed pineapple,
- 2 cups mashed bananas (about 3 large) do not drain

In a medium bowl, whisk eggs and oil together. Add bananas, vanilla, and pineapple w/juice. Stir to mix well.

Add dry ingredients to the wet ingredients and stir with a wooden spoon or spatula until mixed well. Do not overmix. Pour into prepared pans in equal amounts and bake approx. 25 to 30 minutes or until center tests are done. Cool in pans about 5 minutes, then turn out onto wire cooling racks

MAPLE NUT BLONDIE WITH CREAM SAUCE

- 10 tablespoons butter melted
- 2 cups brown sugar
- 2 teaspoons vanilla
- 2 eggs
- 2 cups flour
- 1 teaspoon baking powder
- ¼ teaspoon baking soda
- ½ teaspoon salt
- ½ cup chopped walnuts or pecans
- 1½ cups white Choc. chips

MAPLE CREAM SAUCE

- 1/3 cup butter
- 1 cup sugar
- 8 oz. cream cheese
- ¼ cup real maple syrup
- 2 tablespoons brown sugar
- ½ cup pecans or walnuts
- Vanilla bean ice cream

Preheat oven to 350 degrees and grease an 8x8 baking dish. In a large bowl, cream together melted butter and brown sugar. Add vanilla and eggs and mix well. In a med. bowl mix the dry ingredients well. Add to wet ingredients and mix until well combined. Stir in nuts and chocolate chips. Spread into greased pan and bake 20-30 minutes. Test cake for doneness with a toothpick. While the blondies are baking, prepare the sauce. Combine all ingredients in a medium saucepan and stir over med. heat until sugars and cream cheese is melted. Simmer until ready to serve. Serve blondies warm and top with vanilla bean ice cream and cream sauce. Sprinkle with nuts if desired.

OATMEAL RAISIN COOKIES

- 1 cup butter softened
- 1 cup packed light brown sugar
- ½ cup white sugar
- 2 eggs
- 1 ¼ cups all-purpose flour
- ½ teaspoon baking soda
- 1 teaspoon salt
- 3 cups quick cooking oats
- 1 cup chopped walnuts (optional)
- 1 cup raisins
- 2 teaspoons vanilla extract

Preheat the oven to 325 degrees. In a large bowl, cream together butter, brown sugar and white sugar until smooth. Beat in eggs one at a time, then stir in the vanilla. Combine flour, baking soda, and salt. Stir into the creamed mixture until just blended. Mix in the quick oats, walnuts, and Raisins. Drop by spoonful onto ungreased baking sheets.

Bake for 12 minutes in the preheated oven. Allow cookies to cool on baking sheets for 5 minutes before transferring to a wire rack to cool completely.

NOTE: When I store my cookies I layer them in airtight containers between layers of waxed paper to prevent them from sticking together.

In the fall months, we love buying apples from the local orchard. I found an awesome recipe for a One Bowl apple cake. So easy and makes a nice go to for a wiener roast and bonfire party. It has enough flavor that I never even considered frosting on the top!

ONE BOWL APPLE CAKE

- 2 eggs
- 1¾ cups sugar
- 2 teaspoons heaping of cinnamon
- ½ cup oil
- 6 medium Gala, Fuji or Honey Crisp apples
- 2 cups flour
- 2 teaspoons baking soda

Preheat oven to 350 degrees. In a large bowl, mix eggs, sugar, cinnamon, and oil. Peel and slice the apples and add to mixture in bowl (coating as you go to keep the apples from turning brown). Mix together the baking soda and flour and add to the ingredients in the bowl. Mix well (works best with using a fork) until all the flour is absorbed by the wet ingredients. Pour into a greased 9x13 pan or you may use two 9" round pans. Bake for approximately 55 minutes. Remove and let cool and Enjoy!

OREO TRUFFLES

- ✓ 1 pkg. cream cheese softened
- ✓ 1 cup Oreo cookies, crushed
- ✓ 1 pkg. chocolate almond bark

Mix cream cheese and Oreo cookie crumbs. Shape into 1" balls.

Melt chocolate and dip balls into chocolate. Lay on parchment paper until set.

**(My personal note: I don't think they would last long when I have the grandkids over!)

PAMELIA'S BACARDI RUM CAKE

Cake

- 1 cup chopped pecans or walnuts
- 1 yellow cake mix
- 1¾ pkg. Jell-O instant vanilla pudding mix
- 4 eggs
- ½ cup cold water
- ½ cup oil
- ½ cup Bacardi dark rum

Preheat oven to 325 degrees. Grease and flour a 10-inch tube pan or a 12 cup Bundt pan. Sprinkle the chopped nuts evenly over bottom of the pan. Mix all cake ingredients together. Pour into prepared pan over nuts. Bake for 1 hour. Cool. Invert onto serving plate.

Glaze

- ¼ lb. butter
- ¼ cup water
- 1 cup sugar
- ½ cup Bacardi dark rum

Melt butter in a saucepan stir in water and sugar. Boil for 5 minutes stirring constantly. Remove from heat and stir in rum. Drizzle over entire cake.

OPTIONAL: decorate with whole maraschino cherries and the border with whipped cream.

PECAN PIE CAKE

For Crust:
- 1 box yellow cake mix
- 1 egg
- ¼ cup oil

For Cake:
- 4 eggs
- 1 cup Dark Karo Syrup
- 1 cup sugar
- ½ cup melted butter
- 2 cups chopped pecans (I usually add a few more!)
- 1 teaspoon vanilla

For crust, mix together cake mix, egg, and oil. It will be crumbly. With hands, press into greased 9x13 pan spreading out evenly. (I use two 8x8 pans for smaller cakes) Bake at 325 for 20 minutes.

For cake top, mix eggs, syrup, sugar, melted butter and vanilla. Stir in pecans and pour over crust. Bake at 325 for 35 minutes. Let cool and serve with whipped topping if desired!

> **_NOTE:_** I find these make good homemade gifts, I will buy the foil loaf pans, and one recipe will make two small loaf pans. One bite and you will be hooked on this one!

Pictured below are my brother's neighbors and friends Al and Sharon. Sharon is an excellent quilter, and she makes the best rolls I have ever tasted! Al grows a mean garden and does some pretty good cookin' as well!

While at my brother's, often the neighbors get together and prepare a meal together and share in all its goodness.

I am a recovering cookbook addict (haha)! I love looking at recipes from other areas, then trying them and readjusting to what I think would be better. I do have another recipe that I found in a book from Louisiana. With a few tweaks, I have made it in small loaf pans for bake sale donations. I also made it for our local radio DJ's and just make them because I love to cook! This is so good, so you have to try it at least once…. then you will be hooked!

PEPPERMINT BARK RITZ BITES

- ✓ 24 Hershey's peppermint bark bells
- ✓ 48 Ritz crackers
- ✓ Chocolate almond bark sprinkles

Place 24 of the Ritz crackers salted side down, on lined baking sheet (I love using parchment paper). Unwrap all the peppermint bells and place one on the top of each cracker. Bake this for no longer than 5 minutes in a 350 oven. As soon as they come from the oven, press a second Ritz cracker (salt side up) on top of each melted bell to create a sandwich cookie.

Refrigerate until peppermint has hardened. Melt your almond bark or Candi Quick and dip in the melt. I dip half the cookie and let set, then go back and dip the second half to completely coat. Use sprinkles if desired on each side once you dip them. (I have made some dipped in the white chocolate and the other half of the cracker in chocolate for variety.) Store in an airtight container. The taste of these is fabulous! Very easy to throw together for company or cookie exchanges! Of course, this makes 24 cookies. The recipe can be doubled or tripled if desired!

RUM GLAZED ROASTED PECANS

This is a recipe we found using pecan halves and rum. We get each year, fresh pecans, we buy the cracked and Paul will shell them, and I vacuum freeze them for baking. We wanted something different this past Holiday and came across this recipe!

- 2 cups whole pecans (I use halves)
- ¼ cup white sugar
- ¼ cup brown sugar
- ¼ teaspoon salt
- 4 tablespoons rum (we use Capt. Morgan)

Cooking Directions:

Preheat oven to 350 degrees. Mix sugars, salt, and 2 tablespoons rum stirring until it comes to a boil, stirring occasionally. Continue to heat while stirring for approx. 7 minutes until syrup begins to appear clear and non-granular. Pour in pecans and stir until completely coated with sugar syrup mix. Carefully add 2 additional tablespoons of rum (Oops! maybe a skosh more!) Stirring until syrup returns to a boil. Spoon pecans onto a parchment lined baking sheet. Bake now in a 350 degrees oven for 15 to 20 minutes until bubbling stops and syrup appears hardened. Remove from oven and allow to sit on a baking sheet until completely cooled. Break apart and store in a cool, dry place. This will make approx. 8 ¼ cup servings. (I am not sure we even gave these as gifts last year!) Very, Very good!

The Gathering Table

This recipe is the first time I have ever attempted spritz cookies! I found a great spritz cookie press and thought I would try my luck, and if it didn't work out, Paul said he would eat the failed cookies! He did not get to eat them. I had never been so excited to make these!

SPRITZ COOKIES

- ½ teaspoon no color almond extract
- 2 oz. clear vanilla extract
- 3½ cups all-purpose flour
- 1 teaspoon baking powder

- 1 cup sugar
- 1 egg
- 2 tablespoons milk
- 1 ½ cups butter, softened

Preheat oven to 350 degrees

In a bowl, combine flour and baking powder. In a larger bowl, beat butter and sugar until light and fluffy. Add egg, milk, vanilla and almond extract. Gradually add flour mix to butter mixture. Beat until well combined. DO NOT CHILL. Fill cookie press with dough and with desired discs press cookies onto ungreased cookie sheet. Bake 10 to 12 minutes or until edges are lightly golden. Cool two minutes on baking sheet on cooling racks. Remove from sheet and cool completely. (Sprinkles, if desired, can be put on prior to baking.) I know I will make every year from here on out!

Another good recipe for cookies that have a great flavor and are addicting!

WHITE CHOCOLATE CHIP AND DRIED CRANBERRY COOKIES

- ½ cup butter, softened
- ½ cup packed brown sugar
- ½ cup white sugar
- 1 egg
- 1 tablespoon brandy**
- 1 ½ cups all-purpose
- ½ teaspoon baking soda
- ¾ cup white chocolate chips
- 1 cup dried cranberries

Preheat oven to 375 degrees. Grease cookie sheets (or if preferred, use parchment paper). In a large bowl cream together the butter, brown sugar, and white sugar until smooth. Beat in the egg and brandy. Combine flour and baking soda; stir into the sugar mixture. Mix in the white chocolate chips and cranberries. Drop by heaping spoonsful onto prepared sheets. Bake for 8-10 minutes. For best results: the recipe recommends taking cookies out of the oven while still a tad doughy. Allow cookies to cook for 1 minute on cookie sheets before removing to wire racks to cool completely. ** I am not sure if I had the brandy for the recipe, but I believe you can purchase brandy extract which would work just as well. I also doubled this recipe only because as I said earlier, I love giving home-baked goodies to those at the holidays that do not have the time to bake or to our more elderly friends.

The Gathering Table

My sister Cindy is next to me in age by 1 ½ yrs. worked many jobs and in her younger years, they entailed waitressing. She was excellent at it, and she too can cook a mean meal! One restaurant she worked was known for a remarkable Caesar salad, to which she perfected the recipe for the dressing. It's a true Caesar dressing all my siblings Can attest to. I have made it and tucked the recipe in my recipe box and now will share with you. Serve this over romaine lettuce, sliced purple onion rings, croutons and fresh grated Parmesan cheese. The recipe is as follows:

CEASER DRESSING

- ✓ 3 eggs
- ✓ 2 cups oil
- ✓ 4 stalks celery
- ✓ 1 medium onion
- ✓ 3 tablespoons sour cream
- ✓ 1 tablespoon mustard
- ✓ 3-4 cloves of garlic

In a food processor or blender, blend all ingredients adding a little of each ingredient at a time to be well blended. Once blended, refrigerate for about 2 hours. (Shake well before serving) Serve over fresh romaine, purple onion, croutons and Parmesan cheese. **You may pour over your entire salad, or once individually served, each guest may use their preference.

CHEESE DIP

- 1/4 cup sliced almonds
- 4 slices bacon (crisp) & crumbled
- 1 cup grated cheddar cheese
- 1-2 green onion, sliced thin
- ½ - ¾ cup mayonnaise
- Pinch of salt

Mix together. Great with Ritz crackers, pita or bagel chips.

The Gathering Table

CREAMY HORSERADISH DIP

- 8 oz. cream cheese
- 1 teaspoon vinegar
- 2 tablespoons parmesan cheese
- ¼ teaspoon pepper
- 1 tablespoon horseradish*
- 2 onions, finely chopped

Combine all ingredients until fine in a food processor. *You can add as much horseradish according to your own liking. Cover in a dish and refrigerate until ready to use and flavors blend. Serves well with crackers

DEVILED EGGS

First off, when I came back from Florida for a visit with my son and his family, His wife showed me how she hard boiled her eggs! She uses an "Egg Genie" a gadget she saw on TV advertising and was impressed enough to buy one. She used it while I was there, and I was sold. I never put a pot of water on the stove any longer to boil my eggs!

A couple of Easters ago, I found a recipe for bacon creamed cheese deviled eggs, and it peaked my interest. Following is that recipe:

BACON & CREAMED CHEESE DEVILED EGGS

- ✓ 1 doz. hard-boiled egg
- ✓ 4 oz. creamed cheese softened
- ✓ ¼ cup mayonnaise
- ✓ 4 cooked & crumbled.
- ✓ 2 tablespoons yellow mustard Paprika
- ✓ Cayenne pepper (optional
- ✓ Salt & pepper to taste
- ✓ ½ tablespoon Worcestershire sauce

Prepare eggs, cool and peel. Slice eggs lengthwise with a knife.

Gently remove yolks and place in a mixing bowl. To that, add cream cheese, mayo, mustard, Worcestershire sauce, cayenne pepper if used and salt and pepper. Mix and mash well until well smooth. (You could also use a mixer to make it creamier!) If you like, cut the tip of the end of a Ziploc bag and squeeze mixture into empty egg whites. Top with the paprika and the crumbled bacon. Cover and chill 2 hours before serving.

DEVILED EGGS W/SMOKED SALMON TOPPING

This next recipe is very simple yet looks elegant! I hard cook my eggs, let cool and slice and remove yolks. I add a small amount of mayo, salt, and pepper and mix well. I fill each egg with the filling. I found a nice package of thinly sliced smoked salmon and cut each piece into very small shapes of carrots. Lay that on top of each egg. I pulled the tops from Parsley sprigs and stuck in the filling above the wide part of the "carrot." They looked outstanding, and the smoked salmon added a nice flavor.

GARLIC HERBED CHEESE BOMBS

- ✓ Rhodes Dinner Rolls (Found in the frozen food dept.)
- ✓ Block of mozzarella cheese, cut into 1" cubes
- ✓ 4-5 cloves garlic chopped fine
- ✓ 3 tablespoons butter, melted
- ✓ Chopped parsley

Follow thawing directions on the back of the package. They will thaw and rise. Once the rolls have risen, flatten out each roll and place a cube of cheese into center of dough. You can roll them up or pinch them closed. With your melted butter, parsley and minced garlic, brush mixture over the top of each roll. Bake at 350 Degrees for 10 minutes or a nice golden color. Remove and enjoy!

Kathy Mitrano

HOME CANNED PINT SALSA RECIPE TO FOLLOW:

Home Canned Salsa (taco sauce back in the day)

Fresh tomatoes, (blanched in boiling water and dipped in ice water) Remove skins, remove any bad spots... chop tomatoes... add finely chopped onion, green peppers, chopped jalapenos, membranes and seeds removed (excellent idea to use latex gloves when working with the hot peppers!), cook all to a boil and fill hot pint jars with the salsa mix...bands and lids hand tightened, then process in boiling water bath for 20 minutes. Remove jars, and once the lids pop, they have sealed. (I can at least a dozen pint jars each year) Alternative method; Grocery store shelf. Less time consuming, but not as yummy!

Mom did ALOT of canning as well as pressure canning. I will not even go into the pressure canning...most projects did not come out so great. And I will leave it at that. I definitely give her an A for effort... Although some did come out great... Pressure canning was one thing I steered away from... I found it evil! HAHA (felt being left-handed went against me on that one!)

She was exceptional at canning and taught me well how to follow her method. I will never forget the times we went in the hot sun and picked green beans, cucumbers, and strawberries. She had some pretty awesome daughters that helped her along the way, and not without much humor! Humor got us through many tough times.

We were unfortunate to lose our dad in 1969 to a heart attack which left her with 7 children still at home from ages two to sixteen. Somehow, we all got by. Some tough times, sad times, angry times, but all with love.

This is where much of the cooking and helping around the house came into play. Anything we could do to help make our lives easier and not lose any bonds that we previously developed. Needless to say, those were not easy times.

The Gathering Table

KALE SOUP

- 3 bags chopped kale
- 2 cans kidney beans
- 2-4 links sausage
- 4-6 potatoes
- 2 large onions, chopped
- 1½ teaspoons paprika
- 3 cans tomato sauce
- 1 small head cabbage, chopped
- 1-2 boxes of vegetable broth

Peel and dice Potatoes. Mix all ingredients in a large pot and let cook until all veggies are cooked down and done. Salt and pepper as needed. Use your liquids as you see fit, I would add as needed so as not to make it too soupy. This serves this well with cornbread.

**My sis-in-law suggests Linguica but does not like that sausage as well as chimichurri… So, the sausage can be what you wish it to be. This should be somewhat creamy. I also add garlic. (That is my choice; I can be a garlic-a-holic!)

This recipe for crab cakes was a request for my daughter-in-law's birthday dinner. It was a hit and easy to make. (I have this recipe doubled, which was a good thing. The meal was a hit, to say the least!)

MARYLAND CRAB CAKES

- 2 eggs
- 3 ¾ tablespoons mayo
- 2 ¼ teaspoons Dijon mustard
- 1 ½ teaspoons Worcestershire Sauce
- 1 ½ teaspoons Old Bay Seasoning
- ½ teaspoon salt
- ½ cup finely chopped celery
- 3-4 tablespoon finely chopped fresh parsley
- 1 ½ lb. lump crab meat**
- ¾ cup panko crumbs
- canola oil

**Please use REAL crab meat, NO imitation!

Line a large baking sheet with foil or parchment paper.

Combine the eggs, mayo, mustard, Worcestershire, Old Bay, salt, celery, and parsley in a large bowl and mix well. Add the crab meat (be sure to check the crabmeat for any hard or sharp cartilage). Add panko and gently fold mixture together until just combined, being careful not to shred the crab meat. Shape into 8 patties (each patty should be about a nice solid ½ cup each of mixture) Place the patties on the baking sheet and cover and refrigerate for at least an hour. Preheat a large nonstick pan over medium heat and coat with the canola oil. When the oil is hot, gently place crab cakes in pan and cook until golden brown (approximately 3-5 minutes per side) Be careful not to have the heat too high as oil will tend to splatter, and you want patties to remain a nice brown coating. Remove from pan and serve immediately with a side of tartar sauce or lemon wedge.

Pictured here is Myself and Pam

Going years back, I think so much about my mom and all she did to prepare meals for us. She did a lot of canning of tomatoes, cucumbers, green beans, potatoes and even corn. She attempted sauerkraut and as I remember watching that bubble and brew while in the jar. I waited for one day for it to blow its top! I can laugh at it, but at the same time, it makes me realize just how much she had to do on her own when our dad passed. I remember sitting at the table and watching her chop vegetables and asked what she was making. She called it "Thunder and Lightning." It was a mix of fresh vegetables. I had asked her to make some for me. She gave me a list, said bring these items over, and you can make it on your own. She taught us not by doing for us but watching us do it under her instruction. For that, I am grateful, as I would not be canning salsas, pickles, relish, tomatoes and such. This following recipe is not on paper but embedded in my mind's recipe box. I later found out that "Thunder and Lightning" is a home take on the more common dish: Pico de Galo. To be honest, her recipe is by far much better than what I can get at a Mexican restaurant. I have no quantities of each item to list. I just add as I go and taste. Following are the ingredients that I use for mom's recipe:

Kathy Mitrano

MOM'S THUNDER AND LIGHTENING SALSA

- ✓ Roma tomatoes, diced
- ✓ Green pepper, diced
- ✓ Red sweet pepper, diced
- ✓ Green onions, diced;
- ✓ Celery halved lengthwise and diced. (greens and white both)
- ✓ English cucumbers, peeled and diced (I sometimes use gourmet cucumbers, which are the smaller ones. Smaller seeds & better flavor)
- ✓ A bunch of fresh cilantro, chopped
- ✓ Fresh squeezed lime juice
- ✓ 3 or 4 cloves garlic, chopped fine
- ✓ Salt & pepper as needed

If you choose, use a half of deveined seedless jalapeno pepper minced.

Mix all the above ingredients together, season with the lime and cilantro as desired until you get a taste you like. My mom always said you should let the flavors "incorporate" before serving. Keep refrigerated until ready to use.

I like buying the soft corn or flour tortillas and cut into wedges and will deep fry them for a couple of minutes as that is all it takes to crisp. Drain on paper towels. Salt them if needed. Serve with the Salsa! I go home with an empty dish most always!

She also taught me how to can tomatoes and salsa, and to this day, I still love canning. In the winter months for chili and stews, nothing is better than opening that jar and hearing the seal pop open! Of all the 9 children, we all did canning in one form or another and still to this day I do as much as I can. Here is a picture of my brother in the process of canning, while at the table his wife Barb and my mom getting the tomatoes ready for him! A family affair indeed!

Jimmy at the stove cooking down the tomatoes, ready to can them!

Through the years, I found it easier to buy bushels of tomatoes to can as I don't have a large enough space to grow as many tomatoes as I like to can. I make both tomatoes for soups and stews as well as pints of salsa and last, but not least, tomato juice.

I have also canned green tomato relish and zucchini relish as well, but Paul is not a relish eater, so I do not do that any longer.

I had the opportunity to can potatoes and carrots that were given to me in a significant amount. My friend Jackie and I canned those together. We went old style and did the actual processing in a cast iron kettle under a wood fire! They came out fantastic! Below is a photo of a carrot that was in the sack. I had to take its picture. My mom was staying here, and without her help of getting them peeled, sliced or chunked, I would have never gotten them done. But the picture below is just plain cute!

The only altered thing on this carrot was the drawing for the face!

Prepping the kettle for the canning process!

RED PEPPER RELISH

- ✓ 12 red bell peppers, seeded and finely minced.
- ✓ 1 tablespoon salt
- ✓ ½ cup cider vinegar
- ✓ 3 cups sugar

Mince pepper in a food processor. Mix with salt and let stand 5 hours.

Drain well. And mix in a heavy skillet with sugar and vinegar. Simmer until almost all liquid is gone. This can be poured into ½ pint or 1 pint jars, seal with wax. Serves great on snack crackers!

SALSA

- 1 bunch green onions, chopped
- 1 green pepper, diced
- 1 tomato, diced
- 1 reg. sized jar mild salsa
- 2 cloves garlic, chopped (I used Ortega mild)
- 10 oz. pkg. frozen shoepeg corn
- ¾ can of black beans, drained
- Mix above ingredients together.
- In a small saucepan, bring the following ingredients to a boil:
- ½ cup vinegar
- ½ cup sugar
- ¼ cup oil

When it comes to a boil, pour over ingredients and mix. Refrigerate until ready to serve. Be sure to use equal amounts of sugar and vinegar and half amount. for oil. If you would like it warmer in flavor, use a stronger salsa (med. or hot). Serve with tortilla chips!

Cindy and her husband Bob.

We lost Bob in Feb. 2016. He is forever in our hearts. He brought us many smiles and laughs and never had a bad word to say about anyone. He was loved by everyone that knew him. RIP Bob.

SPICY CORN DIP

- 1 tablespoon olive oil
- 2 tablespoons, minced garlic
- 1 large onion, chopped
- ½ cup green bell pepper,
- ½ cup red bell pepper minced
- 3 tablespoons, jalapeno,
- 4 cups frozen corn, thawed
- 1/3 cup mayonnaise
- ½ cup sour cream
- 1 cup Monterey Jack cheese
- 1 cup sharp cheddar cheese, shredded
- 3 tablespoons minced cherry peppers
- salt & pepper to taste
- 2 teaspoons Creole seasoning (Tony Chachere's)

Preheat oven to 350 degrees. In a large skillet, heat your olive oil over medium heat. Add minced garlic to the pan and saute slightly for about a minute. Add onion, bell pepper, and jalapeno. Saute until onions are limp and transparent. (about 5 min.). Add corn and saute 3 more minutes. Add remaining ingredients to corn mixture. Place in an 8x8 baking dish and bake 25 to 30 minutes until cheese is bubbly. Serve with tortilla chips. Will serve 12 generously.

This is a picture of Vernon Lake, which is where Al and Sharon (as well as my brother Jimmy and Sis (in-law) Barb live. This view is where the neighbors go Swimming to cool off before the bbq's get going!

The Gathering Table

Here are a few photos of times we spent in LA with my brother and the neighbors. Food is the gathering theme! Below is a picture of Crawfish. This is the first time I went to a Crawfish boil! It was amazingly delish! Crawfish, boiled with corn on the cob and potatoes!

These were taken in March of 2016. My brother looking towards the flooded lake from his deck. The bottom picture is the driveway to his home. Luckily all water receded.

I know the pictures of the flood has nothing to do with cooking, but what it does tell us that it is times like this, the little neighborhood comes together to make sure everyone and everything is ok.

SPINACH AND ARTICHOKE DIP

- ✓ 14 oz. jar artichokes (drained & chopped)
- ✓ 10 oz. frozen spinach (drained and chopped)
- ✓ ¾ cup Parmesan cheese
- ✓ ¾ cup mayonnaise
- ✓ ½ cup shredded mozzarella cheese
- ✓ ½ teaspoon garlic powder

Mix all ingredients together well. Put in appropriately sized casserole dish and bake in a 350-degree oven for 20 minutes. Serves great with a hearty cracker or dipping chips.

When I met my husband Paul, and as I said he is from Massachusetts and knows his seafood well. I, being a Midwest girl from Illinois the only clams I had ever had were fried clams and canned clam chowder. When we went to dinner with his Uncle Doug and Aunt Helen, it was a place in Maine named "The Lobster Shack," I believe. I said I would have the fried clam strips and I think the earth stood still for a moment. I had never until that time, realized that there was such a thing as "Whole Belly Clams." Needless to say, I was a little apprehensive about eating anything with a "belly" on it, but I was a trooper and ordered "Whole Belly Clams." What an OMG moment! The best I had ever had. I was in clam heaven! To this day (since 2003) I have never ordered "clam strips" again! I did search and found an amazing Clam "Chowda" recipe that Paul approved of, and I will share with you.

Enjoy this if you decide to bring New England to the Midwest!

THICK & CREAMY NEW ENGLAND CLAM CHOWDER

- 6-7 slices of bacon, cut into small pieces
- 1 medium onion, chopped
- 2-3 (5 oz.) cans baby clams (whole) with juice reserved
- 6-7 potatoes, pared and cubed
- 2 (10 oz.) cans cream of celery soup
- 1 cup heavy cream
- 1 cup milk
- 1 tablespoon butter
- 1 teaspoon dried dill weed

Add bacon to saucepan and cook over medium-low heat until crispy. Add onions and cook until translucent. Add the reserved clam juice **I will sometimes buy a separate can of clam juice for the added flavor** Add diced potatoes. Cover and cook until potatoes are fork tender, about 15-20 minutes. Stir occasionally, so potatoes do not stick. Add clams, heavy cream, milk, soup, and dill weed.

Add butter and let melt into chowder. Simmer for about 30-45 minutes or until thickened. Be sure to stir occasionally to prevent any sticking.

Serves approx. 4-6. Feel free to add an additional can of baby clams if so desired! A FEEL GOOD CHOWDA!

This is even more amazing if served in a bread bowl

The following recipe is from a family friend, she would make this and bring it to one of our office parties, and it was a sensation. I never have anything to put those small crock pots to use with until I got this recipe! It puts a Reuben sandwich in a whole new light! My husband, who is not a fan of sauerkraut even likes it!

WARM REUBEN DIP

- 6 pkg. Buddig corned beef, cubed
- 2 pkg. 8oz. cream cheese softened
- 2 cups Hellman's mayonnaise
- 1 cup shredded mozzarella cheese
- 1 cup shredded Swiss cheese
- 1-15 oz. can sauerkraut, rinsed and drained

Mix all ingredients together and warm in a small crockpot. Stir well to mix all ingredients well while warming. Serves well with party size cocktail rye bread, or Triscuit crackers as well.

The Gathering Table

From time to time, as I get ready to cook, I find I don't have a required spice that I need for the dish. In my searches, I created this handy chart for replacing this spice for that to closely match flavors! Keep this handy! I have it taped to my pantry door for quick reference!

SPICE REPLACEMENTS

- Replace Allspice with Cinnamon, Nutmeg, Cloves, Mace
- Replace Aniseed with Fennel Seed or Anise extract
- Replace Basil with Oregano or Thyme
- Replace Cardamom with Ginger
- Replace Chili Powder with Hot Sauce PLUS Oregano & Cumin
- Replace Chives with Green Onion or Leek
- Replace Cinnamon with Nutmeg or Allspice
- Replace Cloves with Allspice, Cinnamon or Nutmeg
- Replace Cumin with Chili Powder
- Replace Ginger with Allspice, Cinnamon, Mace or Nutmeg
- Replace Italian Seasoning with a Blend of Basil, Oregano, Rosemary and Ground Red Pepper
- Replace Marjoram with Basil, Thyme or Savory
- Replace Mint with Basil, Marjoram or Rosemary
- Replace Nutmeg with Cinnamon or Ginger
- Replace Oregano with Thyme or Basil
- Replace Poultry Seasoning with Sage PLUS Thyme, Marjoram, Savory, black pepper and Rosemary
- Replace Red Pepper with Dash Hot Sauce or Black Pepper
- Replace Rosemary with Thyme, Tarragon or Savory
- Replace Sage with Poultry Seasoning, Savory, Marjoram or Rosemary
- Replace Thyme with Basil, Marjoram, Oregano or Savory

MEASURING GUIDE

I am also including a kitchen measurement chart for a good reference! I use it when I am not too sure of what is equal to what! (Bad math skills? Haha.)

1 Tbsp. is equal to 3 tsp.

1/16 C. is equal to 1 Tbsp.

1/8 C. is equal to 2 Tbsp.

1/6 C. is equal to 2 Tbsp. + 2tsp.

¼ C. is equal to 4 Tbsp.

1/3 C. is equal to 5 Tbsp. + 1tsp.

3/8 C. is equal to 6 Tbsp.

½ C. is equal to 8 Tbsp.

2/3 C. is equal to 10 Tbsp. + 2 tsp.

¾ C. is equal to 12 Tbsp.

1 C. is equal to 48 tsp. OR 16 Tbsp.

8 fl. Oz. is equal to 1 Cup

1 Pint is equal to 2 Cups

1 Quart is equal to 2 Pints

4 C. is equal to 1 Quart

1 Gallon is equal to 4 Quarts

16 Oz. is equal to 1 Lb.

I do not have metric conversions at my disposal. If I need them, I find internet friendly sites for conversion tables.

HOLIDAY HAPPINESS

My son, Matt is no stranger to the Kitchen or the grill for that matter. He loves to cook, barbeque, and try new recipes and re-invent old ones. Usually, every Thanksgiving since he and Madonna were married, they took on the task of hosting Thanksgiving for the parents! Of course, I, Mamma Kathy make the butternut squash casserole and maybe a pie or two, and Mamma Debbie brings awesome desserts and is there in the morning as Madonna's assistant. We always had the traditional roasted turkey. Last year Matthew bought a turkey fryer and thought he would try his hand at deep fried turkey. It came out pretty good for a first time try. This is a picture of Matt and Paul (my husband) tending to the turkey! I also brought over a "special" apron for Debbie to wear. Fun is in our blood! NOTE: I cannot even tell you how to deep fry a turkey! All I know is we ate it! Madonna as well dives right in! Her homemade stuffing is incredible! Green bean casserole is just right. She and Matt are a great pair in the kitchen!

Chef Matt & Paul 1st ever deep-fried turkey

Our Thanksgiving Day starts early, and by the time we have all the pre-meal snacks such as rye bread and dill dip, veggie tray with dip and other dips and chips, we sometimes forget to leave extra room for the main course! Then after dinner and relaxing, it's off to home we go, and we ladies get our early start on "Black Friday" shopping! What a wonderful time of the year to spend with those we love!

This next portion of my recipes is probably the last, but certainly not the least. I love doing Christmas baking, and I love giving the edible gifts to friends and family. I extended my baking to include more cookie recipes than I usually make, and they were a success. I rarely keep much of the sweets here at home for us. I do make sure I keep enough to keep Paul happy and something sweet to snack on!

Pictured above, On Christmas 2013, Pam, Myself, Dusty (Friend), Janet and Judy. In front are 2 of my nieces, Heather and Alicia.

Janet, who owns and operates CompuStitch in Highland, made us these aprons! She works around the clock in her shop during the Holidays, besides hosting Christmas Celebration every year!

I can honestly say this past holiday season (2016) was one of the best baking seasons I had. I put a lot more on the list, and I had FUN with what I was doing. Chrissy and her "elves" at Ten Pin Antique Mall were surprised when they had their Christmas open house weekend, and I showed up with plates of goodies baked from my own oven! To put humor in the baking!

We all got aprons and spoons from my sister Janet

She (Janet) is busy at Computstitch in Highland 24/7!

The Gathering Table

My dear friend Chrissy and Santa!(who is under that jolly white beard?)

My first and probably most requested recipe for the holiday season is White Christmas. Again, it's one of those recipes that I am not sure where I got it, but have had it for years! Each year I make it, the batches become bigger and bigger!

WHITE CHRISTMAS

- 1- box Cheerios
- 1- box Rice Chex
- 1- box Corn Chex
- 2- 16 oz. jars dry roasted peanuts
- 1 large bag small twist pretzels, broken into pieces (I prefer Snyder's)
- 2 or more large bag M&M's Christmas blend (red & green)
- 3 pkgs. white almond bark.

You'll need a large bowl (I use those HUGE plastic tubs purchased at Wal-Mart that are available for Halloween or Christmas) **these are NOT Totes** they are about 3 ft. or less in diameter and have open handles on each side. If you do not have anything that large, you can cut the recipe into smaller batches as needed.

In the large bowl, combine cereal, peanuts, pretzel pieces, M&M candies and dry roasted peanuts. Mix together well. In a large double boiler or saucepan with a pan of water underneath, cooking on low heat, add almond bark. Keep stirring until all white chocolate is melted and creamy. DO NOT BOIL. I set up a 6ft. folding table and tape waxed paper over the entire area prior to preparing. When the bark is all mixed in add the dry ingredients *TWO PAIR OF HANDS IS IDEAL FOR THIS. ALMOND BARK WILL BE VERY WARM WHEN POURING. (I found that using latex gloves is the best way to mix well!) Spread out in a single layer on the waxed paper-covered table. If I can find it, I buy the edible glitter, and you sprinkle that over the mixture as soon as you spread it out. It does not all stick but gives it a glistening look. HINT: Locally, I find it at Tootsie's bake shop in Belleville, IL. When I do find it, I buy several at a time to have on hand. It is not a necessity, but an added finisher. Allow the candy to set and dry. Again, with gloves on start breaking it into pieces and fill gallon-sized freezer bags to store it in, as well as quart size. It stores well and does not have to be refrigerated. It goes too fast!

Once you give this as a gift, you will be expected to give it each year! It's scrumptious and addicting when you start eating it. Feel free to cut the recipe to make smaller amounts as necessary. (Especially, if doing this alone.)

The Gathering Table

So, as you see, cooking is a family tradition for which I am thankful for all the memories and love that come along with cooking. It has been a true trip down memory lane writing this cookbook. Many smiles and stories with my family in the process! I am glad to have shared with you my photos, stories, and recipes. My hope is for you to find those special memories of your own that come from the past.

I also look forward to sharing even more recipes, stories and pictures in the future! From my kitchen to yours, Happy Cooking!

Kathy Mitrano

ABOUT THE AUTHOR

I grew up in a large family with three brothers and five sisters! My father was a Navy man and spent most of those years on the ship. My mother had her hands full during those times. I was the second youngest out of the nine children. Our lives were forever full of laughter, tears, scrapes and most importantly, imagination! I have always loved to read and write in journals, my diary of sorts. We were all taught by either my mom or dad on how to cook or be the second set of hands mom needed. As I became an adult and a mother myself, I had some knowledge of how to cook a decent meal! I started a cookbook collection, and I would go from beginning to end and read the recipes and then dog ear that page. Once I made each recipe, I, of course, made my notes in it or would put a huge X on it, which of course meant Nope! Won't make that again! I absolutely love to cook and bake and proudly serve to my family. I feel a sense of accomplishment when serving my guests. I am not a "formal" cook, but at the same time, I love that we sit around the dinner table, join hands and say grace and dig in! I have one amazing son and his beautiful wife. I have also been blessed with three awesome grandchildren. My grandsons are identical twins at age 10 and a beautiful granddaughter who turned 14 this year! The amazing thing is they still love coming to Grandma Kathy's and spending nights. I encourage them to not be afraid to help make the meal. I am blessed to have my husband, Paul, my siblings, my son Matt and his family and my friends as well for they all encourage me and give me the inspiration to try new recipes, concoct my versions. They are my biggest fans as well as my honest critics. I hope you find joy in my first cookbook as well as coming to know me through my recipes. And with that in mind, I found that The Gathering Table fit well for my title.

www.ingramcontent.com/pod-product-compliance
Lightning Source LLC
Chambersburg PA
CBHW041220240426
43661CB00012B/1092